PRA(

PRACTICAL
OCCULTISM

A COURSE OF LECTURES

First Edition 1888
J.J Morse

New Edition 2019
Edited by Tarl Warwick

COPYRIGHT AND DISCLAIMER

FOREWORD

The following little book is a collection of lectures dating to the end of the 19th century and involved with occultism. Some of the material here is of great interest- potentially to the religious history buff as much as to the actual occultist, for its treatment of mediumship as well as concepts such as Hell and demons (which it lambastes as superstition.) Personal opinions aside, it is an enlightened work, one which expresses succinctly the potential psychological risks of practicing mediumship (although it does not take this further.)

While this work is partially, technically speaking, a how-to work, it is predominantly an academic overview- a broad one- dealing with spiritualism in the general sense. Its final section is perhaps the most helpful to a modern audience, answering some basic questions, for example about the perceived risks of mediumship, and misconceptions regarding demons.

This edition of "Practical Occultism" has been carefully edited for word usage and format. Care has been taken to retain all original intent and meaning.

PROLEGOMENA

The educational and reformatory movement called Modern Spiritualism has, in its inherent many-sidedness, developed variant phases of expression and action. Coming in contact with individualities of almost every conceivable character, it has been variously interpreted and directed; and candor compels the assertion, that not at all times has the interpretation and direction given it been of the wisest and best. In some instances its facts and truths- fraught with such momentous consequence to humanity for good or ill, according to the manner of their use by those to whom they come- have been perverted to unwise or harmful ends and uses- sometimes in ignorance, and at other times through conscious misapplication thereof for selfish or evil purposes.

One of the more conspicuous of these perversions- especially during the last decade- has been the growing tendency, on the part of a portion of the adherents of the Spiritual Philosophy, to introduce into that philosophy sundry elements pertaining to the mysticisms of ancient and modern times. Certain of the inspirational speakers, and others among the public workers for Spiritualism, together with many of its followers in the private walks of life, have been misled, to a greater or less degree, by the current idealisms, transcendentalisms, and fanciful conceits, born of crude speculations and nurtured by spurious philosophies and pseudo-science. Sound philosophy and genuine science, while in accord with the demonstrated truths of Modern Spiritualism, have neither lot nor part in any of the mutually-antagonistic and ever-conflicting forms of mysticism with which the world has been and still is cursed; including all those phases thereof with which many have sought to encumber Spiritualism.

4

PRACTICAL OCCULTISM

A rational, natural, healthy, progressive, scientific Spiritualism, at one with the spirit of the age, with the trend of the most advanced modern thought, must be wholly free from the degrading and soul-stultifying theses and dogmas of the mysticisms of the day; and until everything of the latter character be eliminated from the spiritual movement, it can never hope to obtain that respect and confidence of the intelligent, thoughtful men and women of our planet to which it will be justly entitled when its complete dissociation from its present perverting encumbrances becomes an accomplished fact.

Under the general head of speculative occultism may be classed all the mysticisms of the present age; and, in contradistinction thereto, the term 'Practical Occultism' has been aptly chosen for a volume of inspirational lectures delivered by Mr. J. J. Morse, dealing with subjects of 'great pith and moment' in a sound, clear, and eminently sensible manner. For nearly twenty years Mr. Morse has been a leading trance exponent of a commonsense, scientific, non-mystical Spiritualism- free at all times from the extravagances and perversions, the metaphysical idealisms, and the rhapsodical moonshine with which in some quarters the Spiritual Philosophy has been heavily burdened, to its sore detriment and disgrace. Having had the pleasure of being present at the original delivery of the discourses composing this volume, I am enabled to understandingly and conscientiously commend them to the attention and study of all those interested in the topics treated; and who should not be? As the title of the work indicates, it will be found truly practical; being rich in instruction upon matters of deep import to all humanity. Its teachings concerning the Trance and Mediumship are pregnant with valuable instruction and judicious counsel. The true character of Magic, Sorcery, and Witchcraft in the light of an enlightened Spiritual Philosophy, devoid of present-day mysticisms, whether theosophic, occultic, or what not, is succinctly and graphically presented. The last three lessons will probably be found among the most interesting of the series, furnishing as they do a variety of information upon the states and conditions of the spirit world- information much of it, I think, not generally known to the Spiritual public. In my judgment, the lessons in this book, as a whole, are sound in doctrine; they are edifying and profitable in instruction; they are elevating and spiritualizing in tendency; and they are worthy the careful, thoughtful study of all.

William Emmette Coleman.
San Francisco, Cal., December, 1887.

The following Lectures were reported by
Mr. G. H. Hawes
Of San Francisco, California

PRACTICAL OCCULTISM

FIRST LECTURE

THE TRANCE AS THE DOORWAY TO THE OCCULT. ITS MAGNETIC, NATURAL, AND SPIRITUAL FORMS OF INDUCTION

Our topic is the 'Trance as the Doorway to the Occult' dealing with it in its natural, magnetic, and spiritual methods of induction, and endeavoring, as a consequence, to show you what a wondrous and marvelous doorway into the unseen there is treasured within the life possibilities of all humanity; for we hold it as one of the cardinal principles of being, that the constitution of humanity at large is practically a unit in its character- that there is no possibility pertaining to any one of the children of earth that is not also latent in all other of earth's children.

The varied manner of development, the peculiarities and idiosyncrasies of individual character, and the opportunities of exercise, alone constitute the differentiating conditions which give to one a seeming excess of development, and to another no apparent manifestation at all. But, by and by, in the progress of humanity, when the laws of being are more correctly and truly understood, it will be found how each and all of you, within the measure of your capacities, in accordance with your possibilities, and in relation to your requirements, will be able to develop all the possibilities that are latent in humanity, collectively as well as individually. Then mystery, and all the results of ignorance and superstition, shall be banished from the pathway, and the unseen and spiritual life of man, with all its qualities and attributes, shall stand revealed as plainly and as clearly to the understanding as do your surroundings in the external universe today.

The Trance condition is the warrant of death and the

prophecy of futurity; it is, in its revelation of the higher capacities of human nature, the measure and certain indication, the hand-post, as it were, upon the highway of eternal life, pointing to the mountains of wisdom, that lie, perhaps, still enshrouded by the mists of ignorance, and thereby concealed from the understanding of humanity today. We are aware that this is a great and somewhat startling claim, but yet we think the matters we are about to present will more than justify it; for you will bear in mind that if death be an impassable gulf over which the spirit can never return to mortality, there can be no sort of evidence presented in this world that can tell you what is upon the other side of that gulf.

But if there can be a miniature representation of, or a correspondence to, that phenomenon which is called death, then there is a vindication of death, an interpretation of its issues, an explanation of its consequences; and if that miniature representation can be experienced by the individual and he return to human life and consciousness again, two ends are gained; first, the realization of an existence of himself apart from his external and material body with its outward consciousness; secondly, his ability to triumph over the limitations of his material environments, and then return to all its possessions in their fullness and entirety.

Thus you see that virtually the Trance, which is this miniature representation of death, gives you the key by which you may transcend the environments of mortality and ascend into the domain of spirituality. It is, indeed, the doorway to the occult- to that which is hidden from the ordinary investigation and outward consciousness; a passage-way from the realm of action upon the external side of life to the realm of action upon the internal side of life; but in every case its opening depends upon your own organic constitutions, your mental, nervous, and spiritual possibilities and environments- the means upon which you will be dependent to open this portal for yourselves.

All life, intelligence, and conscious action, so far as man is concerned, is, as you know, a duality; it has its outward expression upon the plane of physical existence, as well as it has its interior or spiritual expressions of which you alone are conscious. All that your fellows outside of yourself can know of you is that amount of your spiritual self which expresses itself in your actions and your speech; but even these are cumbered, covered up obscured, and diverted, by the external causes impinging upon your actions and life from day to day. Therefore it is possible that one may grasp your hand, gaze into your eyes, and hear your voice day after day for years, and be no nearer knowing you than had you never met. But could you find a way by which you could enter into each other's essential nature, by which you could spiritually come en rapport, then, perchance, it might be discovered that you were altogether different kind of people beneath the outward seeming- that you had altogether a different identity; that there was a better part of you- a more wonderful part, a part removed from the external life, a spiritual part that was struggling and striving, imperfectly, alas! in many cases, to make itself known through the outward manifestations of sense and thought and action. Some there are (more perhaps than might be expected) whose inner natures flash and glow through the outward forms of life and conduct; and these royal souls are among the leaders, heroes, and the nobler sorts of men; and when you clasp their hands you feel the power of this inward something magnetically beating upon your own pulses, echoing in the chambers of your mind, and flashing before the windows of your own souls. But, alas! these better sorts of people are, in the main, few and far between to-day, for this reason: the outward cares of life often blunt and dull the finer sensibilities of human nature, so that but little of this better part of man can find expression in the daily life of humanity at large.

PRACTICAL OCCULTISM

But there is this doorway to your better selves. Not only is it true that you are sometimes as sealed books to your fellows, but you are also sealed books, to a large extent, to yourselves. Let us illustrate the point. You are engaged in a harsh round of toil; duty presses heavy upon you and weighs your spirit down, and you have no time or leisure for reflection or meditation; every moment of your day is occupied, and at night when you seek your couch for rest, brain and body are alike too tired to think or meditate, and you welcome as the best relief the oblivion sleep can give. But, by and by, there comes a time when your affairs change and you can rest, and then you begin to think; reflection asserts her power, meditation becomes frequent, loving influences brood upon your soul; and straightway you begin to realize there are faculties, powers, and possibilities in your nature that you have scarcely ever dreamed of before.

Instinctively there is borne into your consciousness the understanding of a better part, and you wonder how it is that this spiritual part has been voiceless for all the preceding years. Sometimes this voice is called forth by what is called religious conviction; sometimes it arises simply out of enthusiasm for a noble purpose, or an interest in some great cause may kindle it into action. With nearly all mankind there is some time in their lives when this part asserts itself. Let us urge you by every power of persuasion not to hide this better part, but to obey its impulses, to cultivate its powers, and seek henceforth to rule your lives intelligently in harmony therewith.

What is meant by the statement that the Trance is the doorway to the Occult? It is really the method by which you are enabled to solve the problem of death without dying, to come face to face with the realities of the immortal life without actually becoming an entity living therein. Is this true? Our answer is yes; for experience abundantly substantiates it. The methods of induction by which the trance can be established relate to the possibilities of a person inducing that state in themselves by themselves; to the possibility of that state being induced by another person upon them; and lastly, to the possibility of that state being induced by persons not living in the world wherein the entranced person lives. These give us, as you will see, the natural, magnetic, and spiritual forms of induction.

The last form might be disputed by those who are unacquainted with spiritual, psychological, or occult matters; because, they will urge, how can it be possible that a being living in another grade of life altogether invisible and unseen to us can induce a psychological condition upon a person living in this world; there is no relationship, and therefore there can be no influence exerted. This argument is fallacious; it discloses ignorance rather than knowledge; for if, as we shall presently see, there is this other part of man just referred to, this spiritual side of his nature, then that spiritual side must of necessity be related to, and will present a plane or point of contact for, the unseen inhabitants of the inner life, when they desire to produce the outward physiological effect denominated the trance.

What are the first conditions to create that receptive and responsive condition in the human structure by which the trance in any form is rendered possible? In the first place, let us turn our glance to the physical conditions. The trance depends much more upon this than is usually supposed. It is generally thought that you must be willing to be entranced and desire it, but this is not all the question. It depends also to a large extent upon the physical conditions; and if those conditions are in a state of irritation, that irritation will certainly react upon the mental condition, and the passivity requested will be to that extent destroyed. Therefore, the first condition we would insist upon is the nearest possible approach to physical healthfulness. We know it is commonly urged that the trance is an abnormal condition, and that therefore the subject should be more or less in an abnormal condition of health; it is pointed out that numbers of the magnetic and spiritual subjects are persons whose health would not be considered good, and from that has arisen the argument that all subjects must necessarily be persons of abnormal health. This, as a general proposition, however, is radically wrong; that it is so in many cases today, we are prepared to admit; but, we repeat, it is radically wrong. The highest requirements of the human organism can only be attained when that organism is in its highest condition of health, and when harmoniously operating in every department. The highest condition of health does not mean a gross physical man where all the mental and spiritual growth is sacrificed to a splendid animal body.

A perfect condition of physical health is cleanliness and harmoniousness in every department. Therefore the stomach, the liver, the various departments of the internal viscera, the circulation of the blood, the blood itself, the heart and lungs, and all the vital organism should be in that perfectly clean and healthy state wherein the individual realizes the fullest and completest benefits from being alive. When this is established the first step has been taken. We need not remind you that all that would befoul and clog the system must be avoided; that you must pay the closest attention to personal sanitation and to everything that pertains to the well-being of the human organism. If you wish to pass through the doorway of the Trance into the domain of the Occult, you must be prepared to make some sacrifices in order to gain the privileges you desire. But, remember, that, after all, these sacrifices are mostly of conventional forms; you must be prepared to sacrifice many of the enjoyments and privileges that conventional civilization accords to you, and we frankly tell you that a great many of these privileges are a bane to you, rather than a blessing.

Then the next question is the mental state; for physical

health, harmony, and cleanliness are but stepping-stones to mental cleanliness and harmony. Without this condition of the mentality, the desired end will, generally, be more or less defeated.

Sometimes it is necessary to temporarily surrender even the senses, also your likes and dislikes, to school yourself for the time to submission. The apprentice has to submit to the guidance of a master hand, that he may be taught to accomplish the results that the training of the master will enable him to reach. So you, as apprentices in the occult, must temporarily be learners, must be pupils, must subject yourselves to the greater will and experience.

Therefore the mind must be calm, harmonious, and submissive; and when the positive part of the mind and the will are thus in a passive condition, the spiritual forces will be conditioned in like manner; and you will find that all the vital forces, instead of vibrating with the intense activities that characterize their movement when the individual is acting for himself, or when all the forces of the body are in full sway, will be reduced to the lowest rate of vibratory movement. In some places the vibratory movement can scarcely be detected, being as the imperceptible movement of still waters in a pool. Then we find the pulsing of the superior forces in the brain becomes calm, the beautiful light suffusing this organ loses the intensity of its brilliancy and activity, and settling as a golden glory it seems as if waiting for something to occur; then this light appears like the sweet summer haze settling over the field before the evening breeze begins to stir. But if we look a little deeper we shall find there is a movement beginning to express itself; and that movement commences directly the first attempt is made to induce the trance by the aid of human magnetism when the operator concentrates his mind upon the subject, and either by his gaze or the passage of his hands discharges from him that vital fluid which bears the name of human magnetism. That fluid impinges upon the external magnetic sphere of the subject and produces a commotion therein, which motion is taken up by the muscular and nervous forces, and is by them carried to the stomach, the lungs, and the superior organ, the brain. The reaction from the stomach and the lungs produces a singular disturbance in the lower brain or cerebellum, and the disturbance of this lower brain exerts a sort of excitation which, in its operation, affects the upper or superior portions of the brain, and seems temporarily to excite it and the forces therein. This commotion, besides being an excitation proceeding from the lower to the upper brain, creates also a further reaction upon the entire viscera of the subject; for the excitement of the brain is communicated to the internal organs through the various ganglia and the great sympathetic nerve. Frequently this reaction produces a feeling of nausea of the stomach, followed by a species of spasm or convulsion that runs through the entire nervous system. Hence you will observe the subject gasp and yawn, the face become flushed, tears flow from the eyes, the breathing becomes heavy, and there will be indications of sickness and spasms, excitement and hysteria- all because of this reactive influence of the lower brain operating upon the sympathetic nerve and ganglia, and through those descending into the internal organs producing reactions there.

You will have observed that some magnetizers find it best to direct the magnetic force to the pit of the stomach, while others find it best to direct it to the heart and lungs, others to look into the eye, others to merely operate upon the frontal brain at first, others between the shoulders and upon the nape of the neck, where they place the fingers to discharge the magnetic fluid into the system. No operator will confine himself to any one particular method, and it may be that the necessities of certain subjects will demand that the operator shall proceed in none of the ways we have just referred to. But in any case the result obtained is the same, and is precisely identical whatever method to induce it is pursued. That result is the withdrawal of the action of the muscular and nervous forces from their external centers of operation and sensation, and the concentration of them upon the brain itself for the purpose of effecting an awakening of the interior powers.

The Trance, of course, presupposes (by an artificial compelling shall we call it) a cessation of external sensation and a withdrawal of all the ordinary methods of expression, and an opening of the interior perception belonging to the spiritual nature.

When all these results have been carried forward to a certain degree, the subject will be induced into the magnetic state, or mesmeric trance, which represents approximately that condition the human structure will be in when it is finally dead. Then a further process is required. To put a body to sleep, to lock up its senses in the embrace of an artificial death, to seal up the ears and mouth and eyes, is, after all, but a poor process, without the ultimate result of awakening the consciousness upon the inner plane. But when such awakening is accomplished, then the individual becomes clairvoyant. The spiritual counterparts of the physical senses are then awakened, so that the spiritual eye will see spiritual things, the spiritual ear will receive the vibrations of the spiritual atmosphere, the spiritual brain will respond to the thoughts of the spiritual realm, and the individual being thus partially enfranchised, partially inducted through the doorway into the 'occult realms'- into the realms concealed from the outer senses- will see and hear and know and have a rational understanding of the conditions belonging to that which is called the Occult realm of life.

Can the knowledge of these things be transmitted to the outer consciousness, and be retained and remembered by the individual, when the magnetic process is reversed and the locked forces of the body are again sent upon their usual mission? Yes, by the will of the magnetizer the experiences of the sleeping subject (to use the familiar phrase) can be directed to the channels of the mind, to the chambers of the memory, through which, and in which, these interior experiences can be stored; so that, when the individual is brought back again to the normal state, slowly, as the mind clears, and he is able again to handle the machinery of his outer consciousness, he can bring to memory the facts and experiences of his interior state, and tell you what he saw, what he did, and where he went.

But you will ask here- though scarcely necessary- how are we to know that, when the individual is thus inducted magnetically into the trance state, he really has seen and heard and known things that do not belong to this outward state of ours? When he tells you, as he can and does many times, of those whom the world hath lost sight of for years, who, perhaps, have been mourned as gone forever- when he brings you some fact that upon further inquiry clearly proves he has seen the world wherein departed humanity exists- the testimony must be accepted just the same as the testimony of the traveler who visits a distant country and returns to tell you of its people and its nature.

The constant induction of the magnetic trance is an experience not to be sought. Any method or power that always demands your reliance upon it is a dangerous method, an injurious power. It teaches you the lesson of dependence rather than independence; it teaches you to be always leaning upon somebody stronger than yourself, rather than impressing upon you the duty of developing your own strength so that you may walk alone. But, as a means of opening the door, as a means of carrying you forward to the occult, and bringing you face to face with the facts and purposes belonging to it, the magnetic induction of the trance is primarily and preeminently a necessity in the great majority of cases.

Now when the psychologist grows just a trifle wiser and learns a little more- not so very much- he will be able to take another step in his own usefulness, and be able to exalt his subjects to a greater degree of value to the world.

When he has induced them into the magnetic state he will then teach them how to understand that state while they are in it, so that they, themselves, may induce it, by first showing how they may release themselves from it. He will be able to say, "I have opened the door for you, I have explained the nature of the lock upon it to you, and if you will follow my instructions you will be able to open and close this door whenever you desire. The key is yours; you can use it, and the bolts of the lock will ever respond to it."

If another can induce the trance for you, why should you not be able to enter that state yourself unaided?

What another can do for you, you can do for yourself. It is only the knowing of the how that stands in the way. How, then,can you do this? Concentration of mind requires meditation, and a determined effort upon your part to withdraw yourself from external attractions, influences, and sensations- these are the necessary stages towards the self induction of the trance; and when by due attention to other circumstances and surroundings you can seclude yourselves and concentrate your minds upon the determination to withdraw from the external life, from the external senses of the body, from the external desires and activities of daily life, and retire within yourself, you will then find yourself seeking in the right direction for what you wish to accomplish. How often do you do this partially when meditating, or while indulging in pleasant reveries?

PRACTICAL OCCULTISM

There you sit lost to the outer life and senses, within yourself and forgetful of all around you, even sometimes forgetting you are living in this world. If you add to this an intelligent desire and an earnest purpose, then you will seal your outward senses completely and pass into the realm of the impalpable and occult, and of yourself gain the knowledge by your own efforts that hitherto you were dependent upon the aid of magnetizers to accomplish for you.

Some will ask, "Is it safe? Is it dangerous? Would I ever wake up again?" When you have been trained in the first manner referred to and spiritually made conscious of your powers in this direction, when in the magnetic trance you have been made acquainted with the machinery you have to use, there is no danger, but every safety. And when you are thus informed and thus able to induce this superior condition upon yourself, you will not only have the Realm of the Occult open to you in its purely spiritual interpretation, but you will have the occult in its material aspect also; for you will come in contact with the finer physical forces of life, and be able to visit remote localities in mind and spirit- be able to travel the broad world over- and gain an immense amount of knowledge in regard to the occult side of terrestrial existence. The psychological phenomena will in their effects and character be somewhat similar in this degree to what they were in the first previously. But we warn you here, as we warned you in regard to the preceding points, that there is a danger to be considered. If a continual dependence upon another's will and help are calculated to debilitate the body, so also is it true that the continued exercise of the subjective powers of your nature will likely be injurious and debilitate the outward powers of your nature. In other words, it is improper and unwise- most improper and most unwise- to sacrifice any department of your nature for the welfare and especial development of some other department. Therefore, beyond satisfying yourselves of the reality of your spiritual natures, gaining the practical demonstrations we have referred to, or utilizing this wonderful power for special and particular necessities, we counsel you not to abstract yourselves from the external life and its duties too frequently, not to neglect the requirements of the outer world, but at all times and under all circumstances remember that your first duty is to that plane of being upon which you at present reside.

Then we come to the spiritual form of the induction of the Trance. We have told you, by reason of the fact that man was a spiritual being, that, because he has these spiritual powers, he is of necessity related to the spiritual world and its inhabitants, and therefore there was a point of contact between the two conditions; now we have to deal with the point of contact referred to. The spiritual people are like yourselves; they have a rational existence, they possess like powers, they are surrounded with spiritual and psychic auras or magnetic spheres, as are yourselves.

Each one and every one of you is surrounded by a magnetic, psychic, or spiritual sphere; and the character, color, and vibrations of that sphere are all visible to the observing spirit, who can see therein your own spiritual character and unfolding. These are wonderful and important truths; and when you are inclined to deride your fellows, let the counter-reflection come to you that there are eyes looking down upon you that can read your very soul and know of a truth what your natures and dispositions really are. The spiritual method of inducing the Trance is this; and perhaps to make it clear, we will give you an illustration within our own personal knowledge. Granting that we have all the conditions previously referred to in relation to health, harmony, and cleanliness of body, we have still to add another ingredient, which is cleanliness of mind. It is a most pernicious doctrine, that the mental and moral character of a spiritual subject has nothing at all to do with the phenomena presented through that subject. The very reverse is the case; for, when you enter into the higher consideration of psychical phenomena, everything depends upon the mental, moral, and spiritual cleanliness of the individual subject. Bear that truth reverently in your minds; for the counter-theory is degrading and debasing- a most dangerous and damaging doctrine, which hinders all psychical progress or spiritual development.

The spirit mesmerists, being in the subjective world, have to commence their operations from the subjective plane and work outwards, as already stated. Hence then, we have to operate upon the counterparts of the physical body as presented in the spiritual body; and to reach these we commence operation upon the outer magnetic sphere, but direct its effects to the spiritual or under side of the human being. Now this may be accomplished physiologically, by directing the mind or thoughts of the the controlling power towards the affections; for it is by working through the affectional sphere we are able to come in contact with the physical condition of the affectional propensities. The connecting point, so to speak, between the animal and the higher side of human nature is the affections, and through the affections the outer physical organization is reached; and then the control being thus established in the lower or basilar brain, the effect can be continued into the superior and frontal brains.

Then, if the manipulation is purely and solely for a mechanical result, instead of turning the forces into the superior or intellectual brain, the flow of force is continued into the nervous department, and from the nervous outward into the muscular department; and thus, by having the sympathetic nervous system under control and influence we are gradually able to withdraw the outer forces and bring them inwardly, as in the case of the human mesmerist; and thus little by little we are able to suspend the active operations of external sensation and consciousness and induce the condition of sleep that you know as the spiritual or magnetic Trance.

PRACTICAL OCCULTISM

The work begins internally in this case, progresses externally, and then reacts and turns inward again. Thus you will observe the induction of the Trance upon the human subject, by the inhabitants of the spiritual world, is a somewhat more complicated process than the process when accomplished by human agency. We have, to work from within outwardly, and then from the outward to the within.

The condition being thus induced, the direction of action entirely depends upon the results that are desired; but those results are limited by the possibilities of the organism that we have in control. When it is a case of personation it is a sympathetic, nervous, and mechanical control- which being associated with a suitable and plastic organization, enables the operating spirit to correctly duplicate himself in features, in tone of voice, in character of speech, and in modes of action through the organism he is controlling. The Trance as induced by natural, magnetic, and spiritual agencies having now been stated to you, let us point one or two conclusions, that will, we trust, show you its utility. The spiritually-induced Trance is the highest form of entrancement outside of the natural or self-induced Trance that you can have. It is possible, of course, as you know, by the use of various narcotics, to induce the condition of Trance, and by such abnormal means produce similar results to those already detailed. But here we wish again to caution you in the most impressive manner that we can, that all such agencies are radically bad and injurious; they are destructive of the tissues of the body, and they deteriorate the organism as a whole; they lower the moral and mental character and strength of the individual; and if you once become a prey to their use, and a subject of their influence, it will need, in a great majority of cases, a larger amount of will-power than the individual is generally capable of to break the chain you have thus placed around your neck; indeed you will have absolutely conjured up and imposed upon yourself a devil that will claim you as a victim, in all probability, so long as you remain upon the mortal plane.

The spiritually-induced Trance brings you individually into the closest relationships to spiritual personality and consciousness upon the inner plane of life- the individual then becoming, to a very large extent, one with the spiritual peoples of the spirit world. When mediumship is better understood, and the character of the Trance more clearly comprehended, the individual who is controlled (as 'the saying is) will be able to return to external life benefited and refreshed, and freighted with a vast variety of experience and information- which information and experience, in a majority of cases, he now possesses; but not being trained in the character of the Trance, not having psychical education, he is unable to transmit it to the external side of memory, and so bring it into his active consciousness when he returns to the ordinary state.

One other suggestion, which will be more clearly illustrated in a further lecture: in regard to the induction of the Trance by the artificial methods used by the magicians and sorcerers of ancient and modern times, we only wish to suggest that there is a general psychical condition established by conforming to the requirements of the gatherings, where such phenomena occur, whereby a mental atmosphere is created, and a psychical condition established, sufficiently powerful in their effects upon sensitive natures to induce the Trance in their cases as the results of the conditions thus created. Here, then, we have established the fact that the Trance can be induced by three different methods: by another for you, by yourself for yourself, by spirits from the spiritual world. We have found that the induction of this Trance in either case brings you into relationship with the spirit world, with the spirit people, and with the spiritual powers of yourselves. We have found that this corresponds to death, for death will do no more for you than the

PRACTICAL OCCULTISM

Trance, save only in this one respect: death results in your absolute departure from material ties, while the Trance but temporarily releases you from the conditions of material existence, and enables you to return to outward life again. The Trance may inform you, as a consequence of your experience while therein, that there is another realm of being, that there is another self within you, that there are other people beyond you-those other people being those who one time lived among you, and who have passed through the valleys of the shadows of death into the Morning Land beyond. These evidences, these proofs, indeed, make the Trance an artificial and partial death; enable you consciously and understandingly to enter into the Spiritual world, and, as already stated, enable you also on the physical side of life to come into contact with the occult powers and forces of nature. You are thus brought in contact with the subjective side of material existence as well as with the spiritual side of life that lies beyond the boundaries of the mortal state.

Thus have we clearly shown you that the Trance is the doorway of the occult- to that occult which ordinary experience and education declare is entirely concealed, or even deny the existence of. The possibilities we have referred to, as the doorway through which you may pass to the occult, bear no relation either in strength or beauty to that deeper and sublimer doorway, Death itself. That gateway is gemmed with radiant beauties, twined with divinest flowers, shines with purest luster; and when the faltering footsteps approach it, as the outward senses vanish from you, and the outward form, like a discarded mantle, falls upon the floor of mortal life, and you at last free and unencumbered enter in and pass that portal, you then will behold its glories fully disclosed to you; and in that spiritual awakening you shall realize all the bright pleasures and sweet experiences of your mortal life, when, perchance, sleeping the sleep of nature, or in that other sleep of the magnetic state, or of the spiritually-induced Trance, you have had views of the fairer country and mingled with its happy people- all these shall come back to you in vivid reality, as you enter into that sublime and beautiful occult world; all shall then be made plain and clear; but even here, by the Trance this can be done for you today. We repeat that the Trance, either in its magnetic, natural, or spiritually-induced form, is God's evidence and nature's indication of the utility of death and the reality of immortal life.

PRACTICAL OCCULTISM

SECOND LECTURE

MEDIUMSHIP: ITS PHYSICAL, MENTAL, AND SPIRITUAL CONDITIONS

In this lecture we take up the consideration of a most important subject- that of Mediumship. To enable us to do the matter as much justice as possible, we have concluded to divide the subject into two sections: dealing with mediumship in this lecture in regard to its physiological, mental, and spiritual conditions in the individual; while in the next lecture we shall deal with its development and dangers, and some other matters of importance- by which we hope to put you in possession of a tolerably clear, but necessarily condensed, statement of the laws and philosophy of mediumship.

There are many people who consider that mediumship is the greatest possible blessing that can come to them, while others would not have it under any circumstances, considering it to be dangerous and inimical alike to health and morals. We are by no means satisfied that mediumship is either an undisguised blessing or an unlimited curse, for there are so many things to be considered in regard to it that any harsh or absolute judgment of this kind would be most improper. When asked to consider whether mediumship is a thing to be sought for, and an experience that is calculated to benefit all individuals, our judgment is clear and decided- it is not a thing to be sought for, and it can not always be considered a blessing to the person who experiences it. It must always be borne in mind that those characteristics of your life's expression that are spontaneously made manifest are the best for you in their expressions and in their results, while those expressions that have to be forced into activity, and require constant nursing and care to maintain in operation, entail such drains upon body, mind, and spirit, that they are very questionable benefits to you in the end. When mediumship comes or expresses itself spontaneously, manifesting itself of its own inherent power, then there can be no question, that, rightly used and within proper rational limits, the exercise of mediumship can be made a means of great blessing to the individual; not only to the individual, but to the community as well.

Mediumship must be accepted, then, as an illustration of latent possibilities within the character of the medium and as another avenue towards the occult side of life. But the persistent effort to cultivate mediumship, or to force it into activity, should be always discouraged and discountenanced. There are so many other things, so far as the practical necessities of human life are concerned, that press thick and fast upon you on every side for attention and doing, that, in our judgment, in the present condition of human development and human society, it is better to attend to the pressing needs of this world's life, education, and development, than to squander the precious powers and energies in order to develop a flower that, perchance, may bloom a little season, and then wither and die, leaving scarcely a memory of its hue and fragrance behind it.

The first thought we have to consider in relation to mediumship is its physiological conditions. These are of two kinds: the strictly nervous, and the strictly psychical. In the first instance we consider the highest degree of physical health perfectly compatible with the very best manifestation of mediumship; and where mediumship results in personal deterioration or in the destruction of physical health, then it is most unwise and extremely pernicious to continue to utilize such part of your nature, because it emphatically means that such part is being exercised at the expense of other powers. Therefore, the first caution we would suggest is, that whenever and wherever the exercise or development of mediumship results in continued ill health, it is wisest and safest to abandon its exercise, because it is maintained at the expense and injury of your physical well-being. Our ground is strong and sure here. Physical health is one of the greatest blessings that Infinite Intelligence has rendered possible for finite humanity; it is far too precious a thing to be cast lightly aside or trampled beneath your feet. But distinctly understand what we mean by physical health. It is this: that personal condition wherein all the functions of the body are in their natural, normal, harmonious operation; wherein you are 'sound in wind and limb,' to use a homely expression. If mediumship continually lessens the functional activities of your nature, then emphatically an injury is being done to you.

At first, almost invariably, incipient mediumship, or mediumship in its early stages, will result in severe physiological derangement, nervous prostration, and many altogether strange experiences in body and mind, which frequently cause the frightened beholders to believe that the individual is surely going out of his mind. Nothing of the sort. If judicious care be exercised in these earlier stages, the resulting disturbances may be successfully overcome, reduced to order; and harmony being re-established, such extreme disturbances will be very unlikely to recur again. The causes of these physiological disturbances are various. All people are born with certain tendencies, and with certain weak spots in their physiological natures, and whatever psychical power descends upon them will most certainly search out that weak spot first; because there will be the line of least resistance, and that being the case the first disturbance will be manifested in that direction. Is the heart weak in its action? Is there weakness in the circulatory system? Then the result of the influx of psychological power will be to affect the actions of the heart and circulatory system. While, as concerning the brain, it may be that some particular part of the cerebral structure may be stimulated into abnormal activity, and people may suppose (when they know no better) that mediumship has unhinged the person's mind and affected his brain; whereas the real fact is, that the possibilities of the affection existed prior to the development of the mediumship, and the development of the mediumship has only brought to the surface the latent possibilities. Here is a most important lesson. If the influx of psychological power and the development of what is called mediumship results in making plain the weak spots of the physiology, then the information thus presented should be utilized so that you be taught to direct your mind to the building up, strengthening, and rounding out of these weaker parts, that they may come into the line of general health with the remainder of the system. There is another side to this physiological aspect of mediumship. It occasionally acts in such a manner that it becomes a stimulant to every organ and function of the system, and the individual becomes excited, nervous, and irritable, so that people say the development of mediumship 'is just burning that man right up;' this is true, for the functions of his bodily existence are all so accelerated, that, though he eats and drinks as usual, he appears to get no benefit therefrom- the fact being that he is really wasting away, because the great stimulus that has fallen upon him is exhausting his vitality quicker than it can be recuperated. Here, then, must be laid down the law. The greater the acceleration of physiological functions, as the result of psychical influences upon the human body, the more need of caution and restraint in every department of physiological life. Thus the lesson is clearly borne home upon you, that under no circumstances can you afford to allow the functions of the body to be your master; and if you feel the physical nature is gaining the mastery over you, then plant your foot firmly down and say, "I will be the master of myself."

Viewed from the physiological standpoint the results of the development of mediumship are of two characters. If on the one hand it is judiciously prosecuted and applied, it results in the improvement of the entire physiology, in the building up, ultimately, of its weak parts, strengthening and sustaining them, and imparting a degree of excellence of operation and a healthy character to the entire body that the individual had, perhaps, previously been a stranger to. Much depends upon the means that are used in order to produce these results; indeed, so many things are involved in it, that it requires the greatest care in the development of the medium to lead up to the results just mentioned. On the other hand, if the vital powers are depleted, the great organs of the body deprived of their necessary vital power, their magnetic and spiritual influences drained out and exhausted, and they become torpid and congested, so that they do not adequately fulfill their functions, then the truth is presented that mediumship does develop a class of poor, hollow-voiced, and pale-faced creatures that the world calls mediums-people, in fact, who never ought to have had anything at all to do with mediumship.

But there is no real reason why such results should be presented. The only reason is on account of ignorance and the injudicious use of these powers. How to utilize this mediumship properly does not come before us in this lecture; we are only dealing at this point with the physiological peculiarities that are associated with mediumship in regard to health and the general character of the functional operations of the system. We must now, then, take another step, and consider it from the interior point of view; for what we have already dealt with are purely matters that lie in the external. When we go beneath the outward operations of the system we come in contact with, respectively, the muscular and nervous forces of the physiology.

These muscular and nervous forces fulfill important functions, as of course you know, in regard to the bodily or animal existence; and the development of mediumship will disturb them by stimulating and exciting them, because the unfolding of mediumship in every case pre-supposes and implies the absorption of a foreign spiritual and magnetic element, a quickening force. The doctrine of the Holy Ghost descending upon you is not quite so fictitious as some hard-headed people would have you believe now-a-days. There is a spiritual force directed by the attendant spirits that is brought to bear upon the developing medium, that, as it were, insinuates itself into the muscular and nervous forces of the subject, and necessarily stimulates and sometimes irritates these two departments; and by that stimulation and irritation leads to a cerebral excitement which may rest within the brain simply in the external sphere, or may proceed into the interior spiritual department and there produce other results upon the higher planes of mediumship. Now, this agitation of muscular and nervous force will be attended by more conspicuous development of the mentality of the individual than has been induced hitherto. Therefore, working up towards the sphere of the mind and the will, all kinds of ideas, all kinds of thoughts and speculations, may pass before the inner eye of the mind.

Here we are trying to draw the line between the physiological and the mental department of the subject. Before we enter into that mental department, let us consider the physiological in another direction. The physiological development of mediumship may result in the development of mediumship which is solely related to external phenomena- to those phenomena which transpire outside of the personality of the medium, but yet are dependent upon the presence of the medium; in a sentence, physical mediumship. Then we have, first, visible phenomena, associated with mental and muscular susceptibility; which give you those phenomena which are related to the personality of the medium, and depend upon the person of the medium, since they take place within the personal sphere of the medium. Here we have impersonation, those manifestations of individual possession, as they are called, whereby you are able more or less distinctly to individualize the communicating intelligence. Now this phase of mediumship is the most valuable that the world can possibly have today. It is the most valuable phase of mediumship you can cultivate, and for these reasons, briefly: You may have the most remarkable phenomena produced by the spiritual world for your edification and instruction, and as Spiritualists you may be benefited and blessed as a consequence, but the spiritual world owes a duty to the skeptical world as well as to the Spiritualistic world.

Spiritualists have crossed the threshold and come into the Temple, and are enjoying all the benefits and blessings therein to be found, but the enquirer is without the sacred precinct; he would like to enter, yet he fears he may find no means to enable him to do so. But when by the aid of the personating medium he is enabled to see his beloved friends, and they make themselves actual and visible in the personality of the medium, plain to his consciousness and understanding, and tell him specifically points and facts of identity and experience that were utterly beyond the power of any other intelligence to tell, then he has something borne in upon him through the senses of sight, of hearing and understanding, that appeals to him without any of the appearance of jugglery and conjuring that other forms and manifestations from the spiritual world naturally suggest to the prejudiced and hostile enquirer.

Therefore, we repeat, that the personating medium is the most valuable medium you can present to enquirers. We know that in making this statement we are open to considerable criticism; but we still adhere to it, and reiterate that the phase of mediumship we have referred to appeals the deepest and the clearest, to the enquirer, of any phase of mediumship that can be mentioned. We assert that here we have the most useful form of physiological mediumship, and when the individual is thus controlled the purely muscular and mental nervous forces are being used by the operating spirits; and if those forces are judiciously used and proper attention is paid to them, and the necessary period for recuperation that should always follow every exercise of mediumistic gifts or powers is allowed, the individual will not then experience any very serious disadvantage from the prosecution of his mediumship. But if mediumship is pursued day after day without any attention or consideration being bestowed upon the bodily system, and without any attention to the laws of psychical recuperation, then mental disaster and physical distress and inharmony will result in every case on the outward plane.

We now take a step from the physiological side to the more interior department of the mental state. The mental character of mediumship is not sufficiently understood by Spiritualists at large. A great many things are expected of the mental department of mediumship that are practically impossible in the great majority of cases, while a great many things that appear to belong to mediumship in the mental departments are attributed to spirits that do not really belong to them. In the first place there are three factors concerned in this kind of mediumship: the spirit controlling, the mental atmosphere and characteristics of the medium controlled, and the mental atmosphere of the people constituting the company surrounding the medium when he is controlled. These are three very important points; and much of the confusion, doubt, and difficulty that has beset the pathway of mediumship in its mental developments could have been cleared up and relieved by an understanding of two of the factors- the mental atmosphere of the medium and that of the sitters. We are leaving, of course, now, all consideration of what are called test controls, for they really come practically within the lines of the consideration we have formerly mentioned.

We shall have to deal hereafter with the mental characteristics in the operation of spirits from the spiritual world and its effect upon the subject, and the reactionary results of that effect as affecting the medium and the control. Experimental observation shows us that there is proceeding from every individual a certain mental atmosphere, and that this mental atmosphere contains or comprises within itself, is made up, in fact, of the mental and intellectual life of the individual- is tinged, colored, and characterized by all the thoughts, education, experiences, reflections, and mental observations of the individual; it contains within itself, too, all the powers that were born with the individual, and these have to be seriously reckoned with by the spirit world. For instance, a certain manner of living inclines an individual to certain forms of thought, when by natural inheritance and disposition he is inclined to thoughts in another direction; but the overwhelming influence of temporary circumstances binds down the latent thought, crushes it, in fact, and prevents its expression. When a spirit encounters a mind thus situated, it is more than likely that the spirit-thought, descending upon the mentality of the medium, piercing and penetrating the conventional acquisitions, will go right down to the bottom, so to speak, and touch those inherited tendencies, and quicken them into life and stimulate them into action; and so control the operation of that mentality, that, seemingly, a new mental character will be developed as a consequence of the unfolding of mediumship upon the mental side. Then, if you are unacquainted with the process we have just referred to and the circumstances belonging to it, you will say the medium has imbibed the mind of the spirit and become like the forces controlling him; whereas the real fact is that the spiritual influx has quickened the latent possibilities of the medium's mentality and brought it into active operation.

Now this may be advantageous or disadvantageous. Generally speaking, it is disadvantageous, for this reason: nearly all the inherited experiences that you receive by birth are upon certain general lines- general lines of ignorance concerning spiritual matters; then, if the spirit world, by the aid of the mental side of mediumship, endeavors to give correct interpretations to the mortal world, it is absolutely necessary that all the old and erroneous opinions inherited by the medium shall be driven out, so that the mind may be clear. A practical illustration will make this matter more intelligible to you. When our medium was first developed, he was precisely in the conditions we have just referred to; the circumstances of conventional life had forced his mind in a certain direction, but inherently the character of his mind was quite different. It had inherited a somewhat religious inclination and direction, and somewhat of spiritual feeling or character, mainly of what might be called the ordinary orthodox conventional Christian form. But when the spiritual influx affected his mental sphere, it had to penetrate the two conditions-the conventional opinions in which he had been trained, and then reach down to the inherited tendency that was underneath. His whole character had an orthodox tinge or hue; and he would tell you that when he first realized mediumship it was to him something of an orthodox religious character, as he understood it, and he felt that at last he was going to become a good Christian. But having stimulated these latent errors of the mind into action, we, by judicious processes, gradually ejected them, and at last cleared the mind of the residuum we found at the bottom of it; and then, having cleared the mentality, it was free for us to use for the training of his mind in the direction of the larger and wider ideas that we have endeavored to express to humanity for so many years past.

When the mental sphere has been purified, much will depend upon the character of the mind, as to what use can be made of it. In some cases it becomes clairvoyant perception, in other cases it becomes inspirational; then there is an intuitive comprehension of spiritual principles, which, descending into the mind, stimulates it to activity, and enables it to intelligently express in glowing and beautiful phraseology the principles of the universe, of life and being; in other cases, there being organic and physiological susceptibility to enhancement, the individual becomes a 'trance' medium through whom individual spirits may express themselves, or through whom certain particular spirits, or a particular spirit, may continue to manifest for a length of years for the purpose of exalted training and teaching humanity at large.

Thus you see there is the same breaking-up process- the same stimulating and purifying processes taking place in the mental sphere when the mediumistic development reaches this department, as have taken place in the physiological department; and the result in both cases, where the mediumship is judiciously developed and carefully prosecuted, is the establishment of mental harmony, order, peace, and stability, as well as physical healthfulness; and these ought to be the results of every proper and orderly development of mediumship. One stage further remains for our consideration, which is the spiritual side of the question. Here we have to consider two important things. First, the effect of the mediumship upon the spiritual body, and secondly, its effect upon the spirit itself, the essential me. The effect of the spiritual side of mediumship must be a continuation of its development from the mental sphere on to the spiritual brain- from the external side to the internal side. If the spiritual consciousness is to be reached, it can only be through the spiritual organism, just as the mental consciousness was reached through the physical organism. Then we have to bear in mind that this spiritual organization is a fact in existence now, and is being elaborated by the human body while it is living here in this world, that it is the intermediate condition between the outer body which is related to the external world, and the innermost of you- your essential nature- which is related to the inner world of everlasting being; it is, as it were, the body of the soul, even as the physical body is the outer envelope of your present being. This inner body duplicates the outer one, and the effects that are possible with the outer body upon the external plane are possible with the inner body upon the inner plane; and when you can stimulate these latent subjective possibilities into operation, you are getting onto that road which takes you out of mediumship and brings you into the department where the individual exercise of your own powers becomes a possibility to you; for we may now tell you, that the true cultivation of mediumship is a stepping-stone to the exercise of your own spiritual powers.

Where it goes on always being mediumship, where the individual is always the subject of a dominant and controlling power, the day of tutelage is indefinitely prolonged, and no real advantage to the individual accrues. But when you can go progressively forward and reach that spiritual consciousness of the existence of the powers belonging to your own spirit, and can learn how to utilize them and project them through their counterparts in the material body, then you open the door of the occult for yourself and are able to perform these marvels; and being able to personally admit yourself into the spiritual state, you can express through the outer life what you gather therein. Mediumship, then, is a tutelage that leads you forward from the recognition of the fact that there are possibilities in you that others can utilize, to the understanding of the greater fact that you can utilize these possibilities for yourself. Mediumship, if you will foster and nourish it and follow it intelligently, will at last place the key in your hands; and the benign and beneficent intelligences of the spiritual world will say to you, '"My brother (or my sister), open thou the gate for thyself; we will be there to help and to aid you, now that you have reached that point where you are capable of walking alone; you have taken the first two steps in due and proper form; we have led you forward, we have opened the veils one and two for you, and now here stands the third already parted; take thou the step with earnest heart and hand, and steady foot; we will help you and lead you, but now your day of tutelage is almost done, and you can stand crowned with the glory and consciousness of individual culture, and the mysteries, as they are called, of the subjective realm are open to you."

"Ah!" some will say, "that is all very well; but we see mediums utterly oblivious to all this, who have no other thought of the value of mediumship than the material wealth they can accumulate by its exercise, and who degrade the higher faculties you are referring to by stultifying them to all unworthy purposes, by pandering to ignorance, and generally doing their very best to degrade the very exalted functions they fulfill." Ignorance is the mother of many abominations, and ignorance is responsible here; for true knowledge never vitiates the divine realities of its possibilities, nor disgraces the functions with which it is bound up by development and education.

Briefly, then- very briefly and all imperfectly, we are fain to confess- we have passed in review before you the physiological, mental, and spiritual developments pertaining to the unfolding of mediumship; and we have reached the last great conclusion, that mediumship leads on to a recognition of the 'adeptship,' so to speak- a personal, practical knowledge of how to utilize your interior latent spiritual powers; and when you have attained this plane of spiritual development you are in harmony with wise and thoughtful intelligences and may be by them inspired, and by that inspiration your mind will be illuminated and your soul expanded, and you can stand up firmly, conscious in the reality and presence of the angels; for their thoughts will infilter into yours, your being will thrill with spiritual forces, and you will be rounded, developed, and strengthened in character and nature, and you can become the healer, the helper, the teacher of the world, aided by the powers of the immortal life that shall work within you, and in all such exercise find perfect health of body, perfect soundness of mind, perfect purity of moral nature, perfect cleanliness of soul. These are the sure and certain results that shall crown your efforts, as you march up through the pathways of mediumship into the better and more delightful ways of true, spiritual growth and infolding.

Here, then, let us pause. Remember all we have said; take its cautionary parts clearly to your judgment and understanding; and remember in every case that success entails effort, for something will always have to be given or done if something is desired in return. There is no royal road. The greatest warning we can give you is, that in no case should this mediumistic development be sought; but wherever it spontaneously and naturally presents itself, then carefully pursue it, and apply the experiences and knowledge thus obtained to assist you in making greater advancement and further advantage as you proceed upon the road of personal unfolding. As we have often said before, it is better to perform the humblest and most menial tasks of life successfully and be a benefit to the world, than waste your time in unwise endeavors to develop occult possibilities in your natures, when your present mortal conditions allow you scarcely any possibility of either success or usefulness therein.

PRACTICAL OCCULTISM

THIRD LECTURE

MEDIUMSHIP (continued): ITS FOUNDATION, DEVELOPMENT, DANGERS, AND ADVANTAGES

The foundation of mediumship lies deeper than mere physiological sensitiveness or adaptation. It is not altogether a question of the external physiological life of man, but it relates to certain essential principles in the nature of man. If you clearly understand that through the agency of mediumship you are able to come en rapport not only with the spiritual world, but with the intelligences who people that world, there will of course then be presented to you the suggestion of subtle and subjective qualities and relationships in the nature of man which relate him to the world that lies beyond. The existence of mediumship is not only the proof, or the means whereby the proof of the existence of spirits and their return is presented to humanity, but it argues the existence of a realm of subjective possibilities in man's nature, the investigation of which causes you to realize the fact that you are actually now expressing subjective or spiritual power- that, in a sentence, the operations of mediumship are the indication of the existence of superior powers latent in humanity while living in this world.

The foundation of mediumship, therefore, really rests upon the existence of the immortal spirit itself; and its developments are the manifestations of spiritual powers and faculties resident in your natures now, which, through exceptional circumstances, are made manifest and visible to your sight and understanding.

Therefore, mediumship opens up a very wide series of considerations. The existence of subjective powers within yourselves; the existence of a subjective source within yourselves from whence those powers are derived, or in which they inhere; the existence of a still more subjective universe to which that subjective or inner source is necessarily related; and as that source is the superior center within yourselves, that universe to which it is related must necessarily be a superior universe in itself, and as you have a relationship to it by the very fact of its existence, mediumship may be said to be rooted in the very constitution of the universe itself- is part and parcel of the orderly possibilities of existence, has nothing miraculous, nothing special about it, but is a legitimate and sequential unfolding of the innate possibilities of the universe and man. This is the very highest presentation of the foundation of mediumship. Let us forsake it for a few moments and direct our attention to its foundations in the external life.

Of necessity we must look to the physiological system of man for the matters we are in search of. We must look also in the mental departments for the means by which sympathetic brain-waves are set in motion, and their results transmitted in the various forms of intellectual or subjective mediumship; we must look for the still more recondite expressions of mediumship in the superior faculties of the mind which are related to the spiritual nature itself, and in those departments of inspiration, of clear seeing, spiritual perception and discerning, and those clairaudient faculties, whereby you are brought into telephonic communication with and catch the vibrating thoughts and emanations of the immortal world- we must look in these higher branches for some of the foundations for the working of mediumship upon the subjective plane. But we must remember that mediumship is not confined to those phenomena which take place within and are actually expressed by the personality of the medium. We must remember that there is a sphere of operation inmediumistic development and phenomena that is beyond, so to speak, the individuality and personality of the medium, to a very large extent. There are, in a word, the external physical phenomena, and we must look for the foundation of those phenomena, as well as for those of a more recondite nature.

For the sake of convenience, we may divide mediumship into two classes. On one hand, the subjective mental phenomena; on the other hand, the objective or physical mediumship. Mediumship is, of course, involved in both cases, but it is scarcely correct to speak of it as mediumship generically in both relations; for on the external plane we have the simple fact that owing to the existence of a certain subtle force- or emanation- which surrounds the subject, certain physical, audible signs and tokens and sounds can be produced, certain physical tangible phenomena be performed- these being the objective form of results. Then, on the other hand, the individual, physically, mentally and spiritually, being actually directed by a controlling intelligence for the definite expression of all the intellectual qualities and personal attributes that make up individuality in its detailed form of expression, gives voice and manifestation to the personality of the mind controlling him, giving here the mental form of mediumship, in which case you have mediumship pure and simple. The individual becomes the vehicle or the medium for the actual transmission of the intelligence and will and understanding of a personality beyond himself. In the former case it is the material emitted from the individual that forms the means of connection between the material and spiritual states, and upon which the spiritual operators are dependent for the performance of the various matters they may have before them.

Of course it is mediumship in this case, because the individual is the medium from which is derived this fluid necessary for the production of the phenomena.

We think you will agree with us that a more definite and correct interpretation of the word mediumship would be to associate it with that phase where the individual becomes the agency for the actual transmission of another's intelligence and understanding through his ordinary personality. The foundation of the external form of mediumship must be sought in the realm of nature, just the same as the foundation of the internal or subjective form of mediumship is to be found within the personality and spiritual possibilities of the individual. We have no sort of sympathy with that doctrine that makes mediumship a gift from God to man, in the sense of its being considered a special gift from God to man. God never gives special gifts to anyone; he has no favorites. Why should he have? There is no necessity for him to give one a rose and another a thorn. He is the Universal, All-loving and All-just, and, by the universal principles of His being, He regulates and orders existence in every department in divine equality; and latently every individual possesses precisely the same qualities. True, it appears that the exercise or development of mediumship to-day is special and particular, but it is the special and particular manifestation of a universal possibility which will ultimately be realized by all mankind.

We want it distinctly understood that all the stories that you have read of mediumship being 'a special gift from God,' and of 'the angels' coming down and giving you this 'gift' or giving you the other 'gift,' or that you must be 'the seventh son of a seventh son,' or 'the seventh daughter of a seventh daughter,' and all such kind of nonsense, are wrong and absolutely absurd; there is no sort of truth in it at all; no mortal or spirit can put into a human being what is not there now. What can be done is this: The secret spring may be touched so that that which has not been hitherto known to exist may be developed and brought into exercise. But this is a very different thing from giving you a 'gift' or putting something into your nature that did not previously exist therein.

Here we have two distinct grounds for the foundation of

mediumship: the spiritual nature and relationship of man on the one side, subjectively; the possibilities of the universe upon the other side, objectively. How can you realize this last proposition? You can only realize it by a course of speculation which, after all, is not so very speculative, since it is in strict harmony with ascertained fact. The man of science will tell you there is an intimate relationship, chemically and atomically, between every department of the universe; that the flash of a gun will produce an indefinitely extended and continuing effect through the realms of existence, even as the dropping of a pebble into the quiet bosom of a lake will cause a ripple that will finally extend from shore so shore. You cannot do one single thing in this room that shall affect the atmosphere without creating conditions that will react upon every human being here assembled, and the vibrations of the atmosphere from the voice of the instrument we are now using not only produce an effect upon your consciousness, but produce effects upon your nervous system through contact with the brain, and through the brain upon the entire physical organization; thus proving that there is a material correlative for every sound you receive, the results of which are distributed through the entire physical system of each and every one.

These are facts, and very important facts, that are passed by without serious notice being given to them, and sometimes are ignored through actual ignorance. You will here see the truth of what we are going to place before you: for if every atom of matter is capable of affecting its neighbor, there will be an increasing effect expanding through all the departments possible to be affected under the particular circumstances. Therefore, throughout the entirety of being there is a sympathetic relationship between points of force, or atoms, as they are commonly spoken of; which once set in motion here or there, a series of effects governed by their laws and relationships will be produced- whether it be from the waving of the hand, the flash of a gun, the shouting of a voice, the falling of a body, or any other phenomenon that may occur. This point, is clear, then; and instead of the physical universe being a series of conditions jumbled together without any inherent and subtle relationship uniting them, the very converse of the proposition stands true: that every condition of existence bears an intimate relationship to all other conditions; and the key note, so to speak, between them, is their mutual vibrations, repulsions, and attractions that run throughout the various modes of existence.

Here, then, is the external form of mediumship. We must encounter this law, or else the argument falls to the ground. If any allege special mediumship is being advanced beyond the laws of nature, then we frankly tell you we know nothing of such mediumship; we know nothing of any possibilities that are beyond the possibilities latent within the universe wherein they occur. The phenomena of external mediumship presents to you certain tangible facts. How are they produced if the two. worlds, as they are called- the natural and spiritual- are distinct conditions with no continuous degrees between them? There must be a point of contact, some neutral point in the scale relating the spiritual to the material; and in that neutral point, where the material and spiritual blend, will be found the condition that enables the beings of that other world to hold communication with this world. So on the neutral line must be sought a point where this can be accomplished.

The organic structure of man is immediately associated with the nervous forces, and the spiritual beings can use this refined force- which, being related through the human organism to the chemical forces of the universe, will form a point of contact for the spirits with man's physical conditions; the point of contact being in the superior physiological forces; and so gradually descending to the muscular forces, wherein the spiritual World finds the means of producing the external phenomena, the nature and character of which you are more or less familiar with.

The foundation of mediumship, then, is in Being, in the principles of existence, in harmony with the innate possibilities of human nature, is a natural faculty and possibility of the individual, and a universal law in harmony with the principles of God. Here, then, superstition and all kinds of ignorance concerning mediumship vanish, for we find it rooted in Nature, in Man, and in God; and with such a triune foundation there is no need of seeking another, for no better foundation need be sought. How shall mediumship be developed? Here again is a fruitful theme, for a superstitious crop of errors is presented to the inquirer in this connection. We should not do justice, if we dealt with this topic in pleasant and soothing words. You must remember that you are mortal beings as well as spiritual beings; you must remember you are related to a world of sense, matter, and time, as well as to their immortal counterparts; and bearing this in mind you should deduce from it the lesson that there are duties due to this world now, as well as duties due to the world towards which you are going. That condition to which you belong, for the time being, has the primary claim upon you; that condition of existence towards which you are going has then, now, a secondary claim upon you.

Give, then, to this world while you are in it, that due regard and proper consideration its primary claims upon you demand. In so doing you will find ample leisure, if you will, to consider those secondary relationships in regard to the world towards which you are tending.

We want you to understand that the development of mediumship is a matter of very serious consideration. We have been consulted over and over again in very many places as to the propriety of developing mediumship; and we have had to tell many that, as the indications of the possible development of their mediumship were exceedingly small, they had better devote all their spare time to washing dishes and cleaning windows, for then they would be doing something serviceable with the powers they possess. You can waste your time, you can sit in circles, absorb all kinds of psychological influences, exhaust your own, and in many cases become so filled up with contending influences that you are in a state of psychological fever all the time, or so exhaust yourself that you will become as limp and useless as a rag. This is not the way to use the opportunities you have; and you should avoid the injudicious, promiscuous, and insane methods of development of many who are extremely anxious to develop you as mediums, and who often bring discredit upon the subject of mediumship, and do no one the slightest practical good- not even themselves.

It may be thought we are speaking against our own cause; it may occur to you that the greater the number of mediums, the greater the army that is dispensing truth throughout the world. Let us caution you that the development of mediumship ought not to be the highest aim of individual existence. There are duties to be done here; soil to be cultivated, men to be clothed, honorable service to be given to humanity at large; some fair and just return for all the privileges and advantages conferred upon you, which tend to make the world happier and wiser- to build up the constitution of human society wisely and truly, so that at last the divine temple of a happy, virtuous, and noble humanity shall disclose its glorified proportions to the world at large- these things leading to such results being wisely and honestly performed by you will infinitely bless and better the world, and give you a nobler purpose in life than will the development of mediumship, which in many cases has no other benefit or result than the gratifying of vanity or a craving after notoriety.

Mediumship, when it comes spontaneously, is in the

most of cases that mediumship which is likely to be the most satisfactory; and when it comes spontaneously and manifests itself unsought and uncalled for, you can generally depend upon it that the unseen directors can give you that needful instruction you require during its development.

Let us suppose an ideal case. In the first instance, the development of mediumship for purely physical or external phenomena does not make any real demand upon the intelligence or morality of the individual. Here is a point that a great deal of sophistry has been expressed upon. This very argument, perfectly true in itself, has been the peg upon which has been hung the most wretched garments that Spiritualism has had in its wardrobe. Let it be clearly stated that though the external physical phenomena of mediumship make no real demand upon the morality or intelligence of the individual, yet the demand is just as true in that case- of that individual as in every other.

When any condition of life or service is construed into an absolution of moral responsibility or intellectual development, then that service is an injury to the world and a curse to the individual. We place it clearly and plainly before you, that personal moral responsibility must enter into the development of all forms of mediumship. What, then, shall we say in regard to the physical health of the individual? These phenomena of the external forms of mediumship depend upon the muscular, nervous, and physiological forces, and therefore everything that tends to maintain the physical health of the individual is absolutely necessary.

Let us give you an illustration: You are, of course, more or less familiar with what is generally describable as athletics, and are aware of the fact that the athlete has to go through a very severe course of physical training before he is considered fit to race, wrestle, run, or jump. You know how carefully he is trained, how his exercise is attended to, his diet looked after, and how he is bathed and rubbed- taken as much care of as though he was to be sold for five hundred dollars a pound actual weight. The very best possible care is taken of him, because it is found by experience absolutely needful to get this man into such splendid physical condition that he can accomplish his task to the best advantage. If this be the case with the athlete, how much more necessary that this should be done for those who have to stand virtually as gateways between the two worlds! If it is so absolutely necessary that man shall be physically clean, strong, sound, and muscular that he may be a successful athlete, how much more, we ask, is it necessary that the same good training, the same care of health of body, the same development of nervous force, the same development of the entire physical man, should be demanded and insisted upon in the development of mediumship on the external plane. Take the argument and consider it for yourselves. It needs no enforcement from us. We repeat that the development of physical mediumship should be always associated with the greatest possible attention to the health of the individual concerned, as well as the strictest attention to the cultivation of the moral and intellectual natures.

When we take the subjective side of the question, we. are told the case is very difficult; we must not allow the personality of the medium to interfere; the individual must be negative, he must be subjective, must be entirely put upon one side. The penalty of mediumship is very great according to this; the individual is not worth much as a medium unless he is mentally and personally crushed down to almost perfect nonentity. Is not this asking a very great price? Is it not inflicting a very severe penalty? You pride yourself upon your individuality, your strength of mind and intellect, and will you be willing to have all this crushed out of sight? 'Well, no, I do not think I would,' you say. How many people have said: 'If I was not made unconscious I would like to be a medium, but I could never submit to have my consciousness extinguished and my individuality put upon one side.' There is the instinctive protest of the soul itself against subjection and domination, and it is a voice you should heed at all times. 'But when mediums are positive they cannot be controlled, they are opposing the spiritual world.' How is that? 'Well, they are too positive.' Can you not draw the line between excitement of mind and strength of mind? There is a very important distinction between the two conditions. You may be mentally all points and needles, like the quills of a hedge-hog, which would aptly represent your mental excitement; but such excitement has nothing to do with your sympathy of mind, nor the strength of your mind.

If it is possible for intelligent spirits to control weak minds, surely it should be equally possible for intelligent spirits to come into sympathy with strong minds. Therefore we draw the line here. There is on the one hand a mesmeric sensitiveness-called mediumship- where susceptibility, sympathy, and negativeness are absolutely necessary; but on the other hand there is that other kind of mediumship where strength of mind, cultivation of mind, aspiration of mind, are equally necessary. In the one case you have the presentation of the individuality, sentiment, thought, and character of particular and individual spirits embodied and disembodied; on the other hand, you have the subjective trance, the subjective inspiration, and subjective aspiration of your own immortal soul, and the inspirations of the personalities of the spirit-world working through the entranced brain and body, which gives what is known as inspirational speaking, trance speaking, and such kind of matters as are related to these particular departments of mediumship.

Now, though it is apparently true that under what we have considered the mesmeric department of the subject there should be negativeness of mind, we want you to understand what is meant by being negatively-minded. We do not mean that the mind should be so weakened that the personality becomes destroyed. Between the sympathetic attitude and the nothingness attitude of mind, if we may so describe it, there is an important distinction; for the best of mediums for the spirit-world are those who are mentally sympathetic, and not those who allow themselves to become mental nonentities. The spirit-world can do as it likes, so to speak, with one of these nonentities, can twist up his brains and do extraordinary things with him; but at what cost?- the cost of the intellectual strength and mental life of the individual so performed upon! For our own part we look upon such mediumship, in the great majority of cases, as destructive of all self control and individuality in the persons concerned. The development of mediumship, then, should be the development of the body, mind, and soul of the individual, with due and proper attention to every law of health, to every law of mental culture, and every law of spiritual unfolding; and a medium so developed is strengthened in every department of his being, and benefited instead of injured by his mediumship.

What are the dangers? The dangers are greater, perhaps, than you may think. It is very pleasant indeed to be the servant of the angels, to have wise and mighty souls come from their high estate to inspire, control, and direct you; very sweet, very beautiful, indeed, is all this. But if you are not careful, rigidly discriminate and exclusive, you may run the danger of encountering wolves in sheep's clothing; for it is unwise to assume that every spirit in the spirit-world is as good as yourself. 'Oh! But that would cause us to become suspicious, and if we become suspicious, we shall become harsh, uncharitable, and unjust.' Indeed! Do you let every one into your house who may choose to knock at your door ? Do you sit every person who comes into your house down to your table? Do you go out into the street and shake hands in friendliness with every passer-by? 'Oh, certainly not! We have to recognize the necessity of exercising reserve and discretion in these matters.' Then, if you recognize the necessity of a reasonable discretion with your associations with spirits while they have bodies, why not apply the same discrimination to them when they are out of their bodies? It is not the bodies that you are careful about, it is the people who live in the bodies. The same people -live after they have gone out of their physical bodies, for the immortal soul is in the same condition immediately after it passes out into the spiritual world as it was while in this world. When you have tested and tried a person and found him true and honorable, you are willing to shake hands and say, 'Welcome, good friend, we are glad to see you;' but to indiscriminately open your doors may be to let in all kinds of undesirable people, as many Spiritualists forming promiscuous circles have found to their bitter cost in days gone by. Unless you test and prove the spirits when they come to you, you are liable to be overrun by the dwellers upon the threshold, who may work upon your sympathies, who may have an exceedingly good time, so far as they are concerned, but, unfortunately, at your expense. The dangers, then, if you are lacking in discrimination, if you surrender your reason and judgment to the spirits simply because they are spirits,—the danger is that you may be deluded, that disaster will overtake you, that sorrow and regret will associate themselves with you; and in many cases we have found that the results of ignorance or want of care in these directions have been, that the investigator has grown disgusted by these experiences, dismissing the whole question.

There are personal dangers; dangers in regard to the health, dangers in regard to the mind, dangers in regard to the nervous condition. The inordinate practice of mediumship is just as injurious to bodily health as the inordinate practice of any other phase of human activity. You must remember that in the matter of mediumship the strain is upon the most refined forces of the human nature, and these refined forces being the most powerful forces, presuppose by their exhaustion a great drain upon all the powers of the system. The exercise of mediumship, then, indiscriminately and persistently pursued, will lay up stores of bodily and mental trouble that will come to you by and by in a physical eclipse, involving muscular and nervous paralysis- in the drying up, so to speak, of the vital juices of your being, which will cause you to grow prematurely old, and utterly destroy health of body and vigor of mind. These dangers may be obviated, in regard to health, if mediumship be exercised and restrained within certain limits or bounds. The other dangers have been stated in the possibility of your being imposed upon by spiritual vagrants, dwellers upon the threshold, who may come just for the purpose of amusing themselves and bewildering you.

One further word of caution. It is a little personal, we admit, but its value we think sufficiently plain to excuse its introduction. Under all circumstances receive with the utmost reserve and caution long-winded 'communications' from notable characters, who claim to be 'Napoleon Bonaparte', 'Lord Bacon', 'Socrates', or other great personages; for in the majority of cases you can value the communication precisely in reverse of the name attached to it. Humanity is so fond of receiving a great name's seal upon some particular communication, that these dwellers upon the threshold, knowing how anxious you are to communicate with a 'Raphael,' a 'Buddha', or a 'Jesus', will try to personate them just to see what you have to say; but when you listen to them, and use your judgment, you will in such cases certainly think these great (?) ones have run to seed in the spirit world, because of the rubbish they strive to force upon you. We would again earnestly impress it -upon your mind that the value of the communication in nine cases out of ten is exactly the converse of the importance of the name attached.

What are the blessings of mediumship? The advantages of mediumship when rightly and orderly developed are great indeed. When the laws of mediumship are more thoroughly understood and obeyed, it will surely result in the evolution of the highest possible harmony of all the forces within the physical environment itself. In other words, it will be found that the highest conditions of mediumship are perfectly compatible with the highest condition of physical health; it will be discovered that the inspirations from the spirit-world are in harmony with the highest unfolding of the intellectual powers and nature of man, and that strength and character of mind, instead of repelling the operations and inspirations of the spirit world, will really attract them and draw them to you; and when you make the best use of them,, when their fertilizing influence falls upon you and enters the calm recesses of your mind, the spirit develops and aspires to reach still higher and purer things. It shall invest you with such personal greatness and goodness that you shall stand up among your fellows clothed with power from on high; and the wise and good, seeing you have diligently used and cultivated your noblest powers here, that you might grow in mind and soul, will feel that they can help you by their counsel and guidance from time to time. It is indeed a blessing to know that your dead are living; a sweet and glorious consolation to have them come back to you, counsel with you, advise you, and help you in your onward pathway as you journey through the mortal sphere.

It is well to have this assurance and this guidance, and if you make a wise use of this knowledge, comport yourself in harmony with their desires, you may walk and live in the daily consciousness of angel ministry. These advantages of mediumship extend into the realms of nature, and give you a suggestion of the possibilities upon the psychological plane (the almost infinite possibilities, we might call them) of the immortal nature of man while in the garments of flesh, and how the relationships between the natural and spiritual worlds bring the whole universe into harmony with yourself, and yourself into harmony therewith.

PRACTICAL OCCULTISM

The advantages of mediumship shall hereafter be health of body, development of mind, unfolding of soul, sweet communion with the angels of the life beyond, a realization of your spiritual possibilities while embodied here on earth, an understanding in part of the wondrous phenomena in the external universe around you; the advantages of mediumship, in a word, will result in the realization of the fact that the universe and man are in perfect harmony, unity, and relationship. Here, then, on broad and general principles in harmony with law, without special and particular argument which is unnecessary to the case, we have presented in these two discourses the subject of mediumship in what we consider to be its laws and principles, its higher import, its deeper relationship; and we give it to you in the strongest terms and in the most earnest manner we can present it, that the development of mediumship should be accepted as a sacred trust: for it is an unfolding that lifts you up to the highest and noblest powers of your being, brings you into relationship with the solemn possibilities of life, links you to the immortal world beyond; and as you rightly use it and reverently pursue it, and labor for its highest and best advantage, it will assure you not only the comfort arising from the presence and guidance of wise and loving angels, but by it you will gain a knowledge of the laws and principles by which they can come to you- by it you will inform yourselves of your spiritual possibilities here and now; but, better than all, it will enable you to crown your days with health of body, soundness of mind, and purity of soul, without which the grandest mortal achievements fall into sorrow and darkness- but when accompanied with these three divinely glorious possessions, life becomes a long summer dream of use and beauty to your fellows and yourselves.

PRACTICAL OCCULTISM

FOURTH LECTURE

MAGIC, SORCERY, AND WITCHCRAFT

The present lecture is to deal with three very important, and, to a very large extent, much misunderstood subjects; namely, Magic, Sorcery, and Witchcraft. We shall endeavor to place these three topics in their proper position, so far as we understand them; rescue them, where needs be, from misapprehension; and clear away some proportion, at least, of the rubbish that has been associated with them.

To the average understanding there is something terrible in the associations that are connected with the terms Magic, Witchcraft, or Sorcery, and the uninstructed or uninformed shrink from all those who are supposed to be possessed of powers in either of these directions. This shrinking is the outcome, in nearly all cases, of ignorance- ignorance of the powers and forces that are utilized by those who are what might be called adepts in either of these departments; for generally people are ignorant of the fact that all that can be done by the witch, the magician, or the sorcerer are possibilities to everyone else besides- to the unfortunate so-called victim as well as to the seemingly so-called more fortunate masters.

The history of the world reveals the fact that the further we go back into the past, encountering the increasing ignorance of humanity in our backward progress, the more of superstition do we find; and as we recede from the positive knowledge and practical evidences possessed by man to-day in regard to the laws and principles of nature, the more and more does the world of life and action become peopled with subjective individualities; and, instead of the ordinary laws of nature, and the principles of being- as the man of science finds them today- we find genii, and devils, and strange, mysterious dwellers in the earth, in the clouds, in the winds, and in the spaces of the upper air. The more we investigate these matters, the grosser and grosser become these peculiarities, until they reach the age of barbarism; when they become so crude and devilish as to fill your souls with loathing,as well as with wonder how it is possible for men to accept such interpretations of the phenomena of nature.

Yet you have only to remember that ignorance is the fruitful mother of error, and that unintelligent minds are the resting-places of all the bat? and owls of superstition, to be at once placed in possession of the fact that the further you recede from the orderly facts of nature and retire into the chambers of speculation, the more certain is it you will lose law and order, and enter into that domain where fancy, superstition, and speculation run riot and hold high court, and seem to present a veritable witches' Sabbath of riotous fancies.

We do not wish you to understand us as arguing for a moment that the phenomena associated with Magic, Witchcraft, or Sorcery, are untrue- that is to say, that such things do not exist and such phenomena do not occur. This is not the impression we wish to convey to you; the impression we wish to place upon your mind is, that the aforesaid phenomena do exist and do occur, but that the cause of them and the interpretation of them, and the means by which they can be obtained, are not of the character hitherto associated with them. Magic may be accepted as the supposed practice of the higher forces of the magician's power; sorcery may be accepted as the lower manifestation of the like power; while witchcraft gives us the disorderly manifestation of sporadic spiritual phenomena transpiring among certain portions of the human family, who are today known as mediums, but whose powers are under the more or less orderly control of spirits. Bearing distinctly in mind the superstitions associated with what is now known as Spiritualism, in the earlier days of civilization, you will be the better prepared to accept what we are now about to present for consideration.

Magic has been divided into three forms, Black, White, and Red, while some writers have added to it also the consideration of Grey magic. But this distinction by color only refers to the degree of moral quality (or the lack of it) that may be involved in the operations concerned. The magician is supposed to be an individual, who, by certain training or hereditary descent, possesses a peculiar power and develops certain possibilities far beyond those possessed or developed by the majority of his fellows. Not only is he supposed to possess this power in himself, but this power is supposed to give him the ability to control certain orders of invisible beings; or, in other cases, to bring himself into harmony with certain orders of invisible beings; or, under certain other conditions, to entreat the assistance and bring down the presence of still more superior powers than either of these just referred to; while the lowest forms of magical exercise are supposed to be a control of the demons, sprites, and spirits of this world- the lower classes of alleged subjective material-spiritual entities.

Now here we have in the matter of magic three separate planes of operation. In the first place it might be inferred that the operations would all pertain to this world's life, its selfish desires, its individual peculiarities and necessities, and most likely would belong to those matters which are dark, degrading, and possibly undesirable. Here, then, we shall likely find all the superstitious forms of invoking and evoking, by weird and strange processes, these alleged spirits of earth, air, fire, water, etc.

Startling stories are told you of Occult gatherings where, under mysterious oaths in magical circles, with peculiar odors, with strange and curious symbols, with many peculiar personal preparations, you are introduced to that magic chamber where these mysterious entities are, and by such processes they are brought to you and made your servants. But fearful oaths of silence are imposed upon you, and you are forbidden for your life to step outside of the charmed circle wherein you have been placed for safety. We have very little hesitation in saying that while the phenomena are perfectly true, the interpretation of them is decidedly erroneous, and that this phase of magic is strictly possible of interpretation in accordance with the ordinary laws of life, both in nature and yourself. When we step out of this lower circle of operation into the intermediate, where the magician is more on a level with the spiritual intelligences he invokes, then we leave the lower orders of alleged quasi-spiritual entities outside, we come out of the spirits of the earth, the water, and air, witches, and what not- and come into the class of spiritual intelligences who are really disembodied intelligences, the people who have lived in this world or alleged intelligences who have never lived in this world, but who in either case are intelligent, rational personalities. They may be appealed to for comfort and for aid, but are supposed to be more or less in harmony with, and under the influence of, these magicians who call them. In the higher planes there is so much that you are already acquainted with in spiritual communications that but very little explanation is necessary from us on that point. You appeal to the highest spiritual intelligences, you ask them to come to you, you desire their presence, and you invoke their aid and counsel; and you do this as Spiritualists, today- as it has been done in the world for thousands of years past.

Now, to show you how clearly all this may be properly interpreted and a true light cast upon it, let us call your attention to sundry facts that you, as Spiritualists, are practically familiar with. In the formation of your spiritual circles you have all the elements that the magician has in the formation of his mystic circle; but you do not burn incense, you do not mix magical compounds and set fire to them, you do not draw a circle upon the ground and mark signs therein, you do not feel that you are going to draw up hell to minister to your evil needs, or make sprites, gnomes, or fairies obey you, or go out of the earthly life yourself, or call down the great ones of the world beyond and command them to be your ministers; but, instead, you feel you are forming a circle for the purpose of the evolution of spiritual phenomena. You are virtually and practically embodying and obeying all that magicians have been able to do in the past; and the real result of circle-holding, when scientifically attended to, is a reduction of the magic of antiquity to the orderly and lawful expression of spiritual phenomena in modern times- neither more nor less.

Then you will ask us why are these incantations necessary? Why these mystic surroundings? Why this gloom? And why this wonderful personal preparation? They are all indicative of certain essential laws and principles that, when better observed in the light of an intelligent understanding of today, will always assure your spiritual circle a far greater measure of success than would be the case by ignoring them. There can be no harm, and possibly much good, in the preparation for attending such circles by bodily purity, both in the outer person and inward character- in the cultivation of meditation, spiritual aspiring, and of the finer and better graces of nature.

There can be no harm in being purer outwardly, inwardly, physically, mentally, and spiritually; no harm in your assembling in a room especially charged with the vital forces of those who are to constitute the 'magic' or spirit circle; no harm to prepare and form the conditions by which you can supply force and power which the intelligences on the other side can use; no harm in opening these circles in unity of mind and harmony of purpose, which enables the invisible intelligences to enter into your presence; no harm in aspiring for the highest and the best to hold communication with you; no harm in having pleasant and comfortable surroundings, and due consideration to the solemnity of the deep relationships between the two worlds, of which you distinctly partake. There can be nothing objectionable, we repeat, in all this; because much good may come from it. In obeying these requirements faithfully, then, you will in these modern times be in harmony with the character of your present civilization, and in accordance with the exigencies of your own necessities- you will reproduce the essential and really valuable part of magical services and incantations; but you will not have the spirits of the earth, the air, the water, or the fire, or any such entities, though you may draw down by these preparations and processes wise and intelligent spirits who have once lived in human life- who shall counsel with you, and perhaps under certain conditions be able to attract to you certain cunning workers in psychological forces, who can do strange things, create lights which float around you, etherealize forms and figures which float before you, make strange sounds, move bodies, entrance the members of the circle, and do a hundred and one things you have heard of in magical circles in olden times.

Here you will see you are dealing with the outer fringe of so-called magic. There is, it is asserted, beyond this, a section deeper and greater, wherein the individual magician can command the service of the invisible forces; nay, some even go a stage further and say that the subtle forces of nature are and can be brought under the control of the will of man, and that there are people in the world today who can play with the forces of being so that they can send this thing and that thing upon you or to you, and in a hundred ways manifest their superiority to the laws of nature! We deny the postulate entirely. Our observation is extended, our experience has been wide-spread, for we have had an opportunity of investigating the so-called magic of the Oriental life, to which we belong; and we unhesitatingly affirm to you that when you divest magic of all its superfluous elements and bring it down to its basic facts and laws, you will find that all these enlarged statements are either thoughtless or willful exaggeration. If you investigate you will find that the alleged performers of occult things avoid giving any public statement, that they shelter themselves behind vows of secrecy, and refer only to the results of the powers which they say they possess; and if you bear this clearly in mind, then half the glory and three-fourths of the mystery associated with magic in the past will flee away forever.

You may refer to the so-called occult and mystic orders of the East- of India, Persia, and Egypt, and other lands- and in every case when you refer to the Magi of the past you will always find them as we have just stated, when not teachers pure and simple; you will find that the Adept has been trained in a certain course of practical philosophy in regard to man's mental, psychological, and spiritual powers, and that this knowledge is 'expressed in symbols and veiled in allegory;' but when you penetrate the symbol and interpret the allegory, you will have the same kind of knowledge that you, as Spiritualists, are familiar with today- the same kinds of facts that Spiritualists are familiar with in this age. But to those who are not within the secret orders, who are not Adepts, and who are kept in the dark, these matters are exaggerated in importance and character. Examine the matter closely and you will find that it all comes down to the laws of nature and the powers of man, coupled with man's insatiable desire to gain knowledge, and the contempt which learning and experience too frequently feel for ignorance and lack of progress.

'But stories have been told us,' you will say, 'of most marvelous things. We have heard of the magicians of India, and others, who have done strange things. Now are not these magicians?' Yes, and no. There is in man a power to use all beneath him or upon a level with him to the extent of his ability, but the extent of his ability is the governing proposition; he cannot go beyond that. The power of the will, governed by the enlightened soul and intelligence, can accomplish in many cases that which seems most remarkable to those who have not been so trained. The ordinary conjurer can do things with his hands that seem to surprise you beyond all expression, and you think he must be really endowed with magical powers; but he tells you that he simply does all these things by the quickness of the hand, and so defies the seeing of the eye; and likewise you will find that some of these 'occult' stories have their foundation in the deftness of the hands rather than the exhibition of magical powers. When we have to deal with the effects magic is said to produce upon other people, we have to consider the Sorcerer.

Let us turn our attention to the operations of the Sorcerer for the 'evoking' of spirits, 'the casting of spells'... 'the giving of life and the bestowing of health;' the individual who claims to do this and that for you, who has a monopoly of influence, who can give you half the world if necessary, or aid you to accomplish some great purpose. Do you believe such things? Do you believe that one individual, made like yourselves, organized and constituted like yourselves, having powers that you possess, has been permitted by the Almighty Intelligence to exercise such powers while here in this world, and arbitrarily interfere with all the laws and purposes of nature and God?

If so, you believe things that are supremely silly, altogether beneath contempt, when viewed in the light of experience and the known laws and principles of the universe. The effect produced by the Sorcerer, in three-fourths of cases, depends upon the fact of the victim's knowing that the power of the Sorcerer is being exercised against him. If you take that simple element out of the proposition, the power of the Sorcerer is reduced in the same proportion. When the power of the

PRACTICAL OCCULTISM

Sorcerer affects a result without the victim knowing what is being directed against him, you can then put it down that a mesmeric or psychological power is being directed by the Sorcerer towards the person. Take out these two elements, and sorcery becomes impossible.

But, of course, you are far too intelligent to believe in such a thing as evoking his Satanic Majesty- you have discarded all such opinions; and if you once empty the Christian hells, you might as well empty all hells beside, and just as well discard all the other devils- for they are of the same general family.

Here, then, we stand. All this question of 'sorcery,' supposed to be associated with the lower races of mankind, is but a blind and indefinite searching after the spiritual powers which you all possess- is one of the expressions of spiritual growth, just as the exercise of magic is one of the expressions of psychological growth, of the power to use the psychological elements of your nature; they are indications of what man is going to do and become by and by, indications all upon the lowest plane of individual development- and when bereft of the superstitions that surround them, they are resolved into the simple facts of nature that in your larger experience you are familiar with today.

We now come to the question of witchcraft. You have been bewitched by a laughing eye, a merry voice, a twist of the hair, a turn of the face, a charming manner- oh! by these you have been bewitched beyond all power to resist; a spell has-been cast over you which you have felt for years afterwards, and you have thanked God for such bedevilment- for it brought you all the happiness you had in life! Here you have the secret of witchcraft,- the influence of one individual upon another. It may be laudable and good, or disgraceful and injurious; it may kindle into action the higher and better parts, or arouse all the lower and baser elements of you; may make you akin to the very angels themselves, or forge chains which shall bind you down to the lowest elements of sensuous life.

Work out the problem on that line. All the witchery and bewitching resolves itself into psychological influences; the psychologist makes his subject believe that a cold coin is red hot, that a gentleman's walking-stick is the embodiment of the evil one, and by a thousand different things bewitches the intelligence and faculties and judgment of his subject, who, for the time being, is under a spell that compels him to do whatsoever the controlling mind desires or demands him to do; but the time was when these things were not understood, when those who were capable of exercising an influence upon other people were called 'witches,' were looked upon as devilish, and, mayhaps, have paid for it by being roasted alive, as a burnt offering to heaven, as, indeed many were so treated. So, then, when we take witchcraft in this light, think of how many thousand of your fellow-creatures in this world have suffered pains and penalties because they possessed powers which God himself gave them; for the exercise of attributes with which you are familiar today, and which pass unchallenged in the community at large. Magic, Sorcery, and Witchcraft, then, in this light, bring themselves in line and harmony with the laws of nature and the possibilities of man; they are "uncanny" subjects only when you fail to understand what they involve; they are dreadful and horrible things to deal with when you are led into them blindfolded, and introduced to them in the dark; but when they come out to you in the bright light of day, when old associations fall from them, they stand out as prophecies of the powers that you are to-day personally acquainted with.

We take Magic, then, in another form just for the moment, involving in this one term now the entire series of definitions that we have been dealing with; we will take it under the word Occultism, and here we find the exoteric and esoteric side of the question. You are asked to believe there is a secret side to knowledge that is only for those who are fitted to receive it; that there must be a special order, a special class of people to receive the secret wisdom of God, and that only these favored persons are entitled to receive his divine knowledge; that outwardly it must be presented in symbols and allegories, and the common multitude who are not prepared to receive these things must be content to receive what the adepts and magi see fit to dispense to them. Three fourths of this talk about modern Theosophy, and the presentation of it in this land, is only pandering to the most vicious element of the intelligence of the nineteenth century. Does not the charter of this country rest upon the glorious truth of universal brotherhood and universal equality of man before God and nature? Take out these two doctrines and the very soul and mind of this fraternal union of different states would crumble into ashes, because the vital soul and mind that bind it would be taken from them. Theosophy shall tell you that there are only a special few who may pass the mystic portals, or lift the sacred veils and pass beneath them so that they stand before the inner shrines; while all you who are of the common clay outside must be content to hear but the echo of the music within, or receive it in symbols and allegories, from those who have passed into adeptship beyond, as they may choose to give it to you. Tear down such trashy doctrines, dispel all such murky clouds. Be not deceived by such specious statements- they are the towers that selfishness and superstition erect to make something that may belong to all seem special and peculiar, and pertaining to a class alone. God's eternal universe knows no common people and no great people.

In the essential soul of man are the everlasting principles of God, and those who are willing and those who are able, no matter what their creed, their race or color, have an inalienable right to the pursuit of truth, as well as the pursuit of happiness.

PRACTICAL OCCULTISM

Therefore we say that all these pretentious claims about Occultism, Theosophy, or the mystical developments of supernatural power are the claims of the ignorant, the deluded, or the charlatan. People are deluded and deceived by such pretensions, they not knowing all the points we have presented for consideration. Our purpose in these remarks is to inform them and bring them face to face with the fact, that whenever truth is divided in two, and half of it belongs to the to initiates, and the other half to those of the outer world, then we say that danger and difficulty lie in the pathway of the investigator; and one of the greatest dangers is a specious self-righteousness which causes its subjects to say, 'Stand aside; I am holier than thou.' This is what you wish to avoid; there must be none of the 'I am holier than thou' in the pursuit and application of truth for the advancement of yourselves and the well-being of your fellows.

Shall we, then, people the mystic temples of the past with the living|thoughts of the present ? shall we take to them our circles and our shrines? shall we again illumine their sacred altars? shall we fill their chambers with odors and perfumes? must we as initiates be put through trying ordeals, invoke the powers of the lower, middle, and upper realms of nature ere we can enjoy the blessings of our Spiritualism?- these are questions Spiritualists might well ask of the supporters of magic in their midst today. And shall we, with the light and guidance of modern psychology, indulge in the wild orgies of sorcery or witchcraft?

Or shall we turn aside from the old practices, remove the curtains, turn up the lights, put away the paraphernalia, and come down to the plain, simple truth, that the phenomenal aspects of Modern Spiritualism reproduce all the essential principles of the Magic, Witchcraft, and Sorcery of the past? The same powers are involved, the same forces are used, the same conditions are required, the same intelligences are operating; and the more you investigate the realms of nature by the light of science and experience, the less and less room you will find for the devils and genii of antiquity.

Magic, Witchcraft, and Sorcery, when thus analyzed and interpreted, bring you at last only face to face with possibilities in nature, in harmony with her laws, in accordance with the possibilities of yourself, and in strict accordance with the abilities of operating spirits, who return into the mortal sphere and produce all the marvels that are alleged to have been performed in former times. It may be said in presenting this modern and practical interpretation of the three themes we have joined together, that we have ignored the existence of the great brotherhoods of the past. Nothing of the kind. We do not, since we are perfectly aware of their existence; but all they can present, all that they can do, is simply done in accordance with the laws of nature; and no man in any case can transcend the laws of nature, but in every case, no matter how startling the statement may be, the result has been accomplished in harmony with the laws of nature and the possibilities of man. Therefore, shall you waste the precious moments of mortal life in digging up the past when its facts are now living in your midst?

Why turn to the years agone, why unearth the mysteries of psychological phenomena in bygone ages, when greater wisdom is manifested and greater things are actually transpiring in your midst to-day, and that, too, in the light of scientific fact and experience, and in accordance with the highest methods of investigation? We will take the spiritual phenomena of the last forty years in connection with Modern Spiritualism, and boldly challenge the magical records of antiquity to produce anything equally satisfactory to the intelligence of today.

Clearly, then, the past may be left alone; let the dead past bury its dead, and let the living present be concerned in developing the life that is, in an understanding of the latent powers of mind and body, brain and soul. By a proper understanding of the laws and principles connecting the two worlds in harmony and unity, far greater marvels are revealed to you. You learn that a spirit can lift a solid article and transport it from one end of the room to the other; carry a message from one locality to another, carry your good-will or evil will to some person you love or dislike; that it can produce a bodily form, as well as reveal the mysteries of passing from the mortal existence. All these things are possible and do occur, and they occur because of the laws of nature. All that has been done by man in the past, and all that has been gained, you can do and you can gain; because every human being the wide world over is built upon the same lines of general organization, principle, and purpose. We leave the topic to your consideration, and urge you to accept this in conclusion: that the cultivation of the highest spirituality, the development of the noblest morality, the building up and strengthening of your will to its strongest point, living a cleanly and virtuous life, are the surest safeguards against the attacks of all kinds of sorcery and magic, of all sorts of witchcraft; that the facts of knowledge intelligently directed shall indeed make you a magician through the forces of your nature for the accomplishment of many strange things; that even as the chemist manipulating his compounds produces miracles, and seems to be a very magician juggling with fluids and materials, so you, like the chemist, using laws and principles and proper agents, can be a marvelous magician in the psychological departments, also, while you are living here on earth.

Live, then, so your knowledge can be usefully applied for the benefit of your fellows and the cultivation of your own natures, and banish superstition and ignorance from the world forever; for knowledge is the glorious sunlight shining into and dispelling the darkness, and the bats and owls so long residing there hie them away to more congenial quarters where the sunlight does not shine so strong. May those bats and owls the world has called Magic, Witchcraft, and Sorcery flee away to more appropriate abodes of shadow in other less-illumined parts of the world than that in which you reside; and in place of 'witchcraft, sorcery, and magic,' put the understanding of the psychological possibilities of man and being- which, when applied to the needs of life, bless humanity, enlarge the field of human vision and knowledge, lift man up into communion and action with the higher orders of spiritual intelligence, who are always willing to help you forward and onward in your progress through mortality to the brighter realms that lie beyond.

PRACTICAL OCCULTISM

FIFTH LECTURE

THE NATURAL, SPIRITUAL, AND CELESTIAL PLANES OF THE SECOND STATE

The present topic of consideration is 'The Natural, Spiritual, and Celestial Planes of the Second State.' At times it is supposed that the second state of life is so strangely different, so altogether miraculous in its character by comparison with the life you are now pursuing, that it would seem, if such opinion be accepted as correct, that it would be impossible to give any rational and intelligible conception of what its nature was like. Naturally, the logical mind would argue, if there is this great difference between the two states- and if the fact of communion between them be true- then those who come to you from that other state can only make themselves understood to your judgment through the agency of symbols and such approximate statements as would best meet the necessities and difficulties that lie in the way. Therefore in this case all statements concerning the spiritual life would have to be accepted as approximate statements, and not statements of literal and actual fact stated in specific terms, and the result would be that the whole of the literature of Spiritualism dealing with the after-life would be an approximate and not an exact literature; for there could be no exact philosophy of the subject, and you would have to wake up, perchance, into conscious life in the world beyond, with the painful fact dawning upon you that you absolutely were not benefited in any particular by all the supposed information that had been transmitted to you during your residence upon earth. If the spiritual world could only give you an approximate understanding of the conditions of the future life, it would not render you any very substantial service; you would still be enshrouded in doubts and difficulties, and the real character of that future state would be just as much a sealed book to you after you had received communications from these people as it was prior to your so doing. Clearly, then, if this is the case, the value of the communication will be seriously impaired in proportion as this fact is known.

On the other hand, suppose it to be that you can get not only an approximate but a tolerably exact statement of the facts of that future life, couched in such manner and method that shall make it easily understood and accepted by your intelligence and judgment, then the communications you receive from that, to you, future world, will help to clear away the mists, as well as dispel the superstitious opinions that have surrounded that future life for so many generations past. In this case communications will be advantageous and beneficial to you, instructive and illustrative of the real facts and the actual circumstances that there prevail; and coming to you in such a character, they will store your mind, unfold your judgment, and add to your knowledge of the life beyond, while they will largely rob death of those terrors that ignorance and doubt have hitherto associated with it. Shall we take the hypothetical ground, or the ground of exactitude? Is it impossible to translate the life beyond into the understanding of rational humanity? Must the information be conveyed in the form of symbols and approximations? Our choice is very simple; we aim, as best we can, to be something of the rough and hardy pioneer, who, working through the tangled undergrowth of the forest, strives to carve a way for those who come after, that there may be something of a road and more of daylight upon the path than there was before; and if we can do this in such practical manner as shall make the road we mark out clearly understood by you, then we must come to something of exactitude, and symbols and approximations may be put upon one side as not suited to the task we have in hand.

We have divided our subject into three separate sections-the Natural, Spiritual, and Celestial planes of the second state;

and the inference arising from this division is, naturally, that man passes through certain conditions thus named, and in himself exhibits a natural and spiritual and celestial character as he proceeds. But at the outset we may be encountered with a criticism and told that to argue that a person passes through a natural condition in the spiritual life is to argue something that does not seem upon the surface to be supported by the facts. We would like to ask one question : How many of the teeming multitudes of spirits are really spiritually unfolded while living in this world ? If they are not spiritually unfolded while they are living in this world, how can it be reasonably supposed, save only by the operation of a miracle, that they can become spiritually unfolded as the simple result of having died? That death will put such people into a spiritual condition rests upon a sandy and insecure foundation; yet you will tell us, they become spirits.

That is true enough. There are a great many human people who just possess mortal bodies, in whom humanity has not yet begun to put forth its fairest flowers; they are mortal rather than human. These people, then, will be spirits rather than spiritual, and herein lies the essence of the distinction; for may it not be accepted that until the divinity of humanity has been elaborated and unfolded, the glorious spirituality which is the perfume of humanity can scarcely be expected. We invite you, first of all, to the natural plane of the spiritual life, wherein all the latent elements pertaining to your present development germinate, flower, bring forth their graces and glory; and wherein all the nobler selfhood that you feel within you now unfolds, matures, and beautifies. Ah! but if we have to take such a step as that, and if all the better part of us that we possess now is unfolded over there, how many of us shall reach the glory in the end, and at what an expense of time, it may be, shall we pass through the ultimates of the natural nature of us, and tread upon the verge of the spiritual that lies beyond?

PRACTICAL OCCULTISM

True, there is no royal road to progress in the second state any more than there is in this; all achievement is the result of individual effort and of personal application. If you wish to grow on the second plane of life,then,even as you would have to labor upon this plane mentally and morally to achieve results, so mentally and morally must you labor on that second plane if you would advance and progress. Now, when we look at human nature we find that there are certain possible characteristics and elements pertaining to man's natural nature, as it is called, that apparently are in the way- are clogs upon the wheels of his spiritual development; and people tell you if you wish for grace and growth, you must trample underneath all the carnal and material elements of your nature. Very frequently we have to raise our voice in condemnation of a doctrine so sophistical. There is nothing base in man's nature; it is only the uses that ignorance and undevelopment have put it to. If, then, by ignorance you have descended to ignoble service, if by lack of knowledge you have become chained, slaves to mastering passions, then those passions are not to blame; but your lack of development and lack of knowledge rise up in condemnation, and accuse you of failure to rightly use the powers that God himself hath committed to your keeping. When the world grows wise enough, and clearly sees the character of God's great government, it will universally concede the point we are about to urge- that in man's nature, as well as in the universe itself, the gifts of God are good eternally. It is not in crushing and crowding to the ground and trampling beneath your feet the gifts of God that you are going to attain real progress, but it is in bringing out the principles that are involved therein; in applying them intelligently and wisely to the nobler purposes and desires of your life, and so bringing out the latent elements of good- the essences and all the sweetness and brightness that man's material nature contains. This cannot be done today, but instinctively the individual feels it ought to be done. This instinctive conception has lain within the minds of men for ages past, and the ascetics and monks and recluses of the world testify to the fearful ends men have gone in their attempts to crucify the flesh that the spirit might be free.

Vain efforts were these- for your natural being needs its particular development, its true unfolding, that these latent qualities and powers may be brought to the surface and stimulated, even as the sunshine stimulates, and warms, and brings to the surface the blade of grass as it grows upwards from the soil; and when you can effect this result while you are living here, then so much higher will you stand in the natural condition in the spiritual world when you pass to it; but you need not think that you will pass into a realm or sphere beyond the first division we have mentioned, for the first stage will receive one and all- for there is not a human being living in the world to-day who has attained such superior development and exalted unfolding, that he has exhausted the natural elements of personal being pertaining to the sphere of life whereon he first commences to be.

In the spiritual states of life you will find the counterparts of nature, the counterparts of humanity; and these natural counterparts of nature and man are the elements of the first degree, so to speak, of spiritual existence. They constitute the natural claim whereon your loves, your affections, your interests, your professions, all that which makes you what you are today, come to you, remain with you, a part and parcel of your lives, and do their work there in your further development, and which fit you for the next degree that rises beyond. Let us go back for one moment. The natural affections of the heart, so called, the desires of the intellect, the aspirations of the moral man, the emotions and premonitions of the spiritual part of you- all these are working in your lives today. You will die, and when you enter on the second plane, all these things will be with you there working with you still; but they will bind you at the same time, for they are links that hold you down to the world from whence you came, and bind you to the friends you love, to the pursuits that were dear to you, to the principles of being you were then related to; and they will hold you just so long as you have not developed beyond, or, more properly speaking, developed up to all the possibilities of life at present active within your being. Therefore, your sojourn upon the natural plane- the second state- will depend entirely upon the character of your affections, the nature of your pursuits; and if your strong affections still bind you to the realms of nature and the people living there, then will you be as dwellers upon the threshold, living actually within the confines of the material thought, even on the spiritual side- remaining unseen, but chained to the conditions of earth, sharing and sympathizing with its people in their trials and tribulations when they are affectionally related to you; but, growing a little beyond this and becoming wider in thought and nobler in aspiration, you pass away from the world itself, from the actual conditions of mortal being, and enter into the real conditions of the spiritual life.

We have so profound a faith in, and so deep a worship for, the divinity of man, that at times we feel that if the world's humanity were only what that humanity can become, the world would need no service from the spirit-world to aid it in its upward progress. There is so much of good, so much of truth, so much of power and beauty, enshrined within this nature of yours, that could all these be brought into active exercise, the world's people would become angels and gods. Therefore, when we see and know them, and mingle with them on that brighter plane of natural existence whereon the spirit man first stands, we feel and know how divinely great this humanity can be. Over there, then, where love is the ruling element, mingling in every thought and urging all your nature forward, there, on really the lowest round of the ladder of spiritual progress, man unfolds every latent element of the divine humanity, and realizes fully and completely all the elements of human greatness. In the main, the majority of communicants, who come to hold communication with you, come from the first plane of spiritual existence; there they are dwellers upon the threshold; nearer this life, really, than the other, they have scarcely passed the portal, and are yet those upon the natural plane of spiritual existence, whose interest, sympathies, and desires are still associated with the mortal world. Occasionally, much more rarely than you think, come messengers from the plane beyond, the avant couriers of a better dispensation yet to be unfolded; and now and again their golden words drop into the seas of mortal thought, stirring their waters with a quicker life, illuminating them with a radiant glory that flashes and scintillates before the wondering eyes of those keen enough to feel the power of the deeper thought and the higher presence.

But, no matter how long the time may be, the period surely comes at last when the latent elements of your present careers are all unfolded, and you have grown coequal with the plane of principles upon which you have hitherto reposed, and therefore, need a larger flight, must have a new condition; for now you begin to feel the need of that deeper unfolding that lies behind the human nature- the cultivation of the spiritual part of you. By effort and by sorrow, it may be by pain and misery, most potent teachers in the main, you have become chastened and purified; the discordant and rebellious elements have been reduced to order and to harmony; and being thus clothed in your right mind at last, wearing at last the wedding garments for the spiritual feasting that lies before you, the command comes out of your own necessities, 'Come up higher' Out of your own necessities, mind- for you can make no advance in the spiritual states of being until the absolute need of it within yourself compels the movement onward- you cross the boundaries of nature.

PRACTICAL OCCULTISM

Of that crossing we cannot deal with now. Suffice it to say you cross those boundaries, and find a new life surging within your nature, new aspirations developed, new relations yearned for; and onward you go, not forsaking or forgetting ail that has gone before, but, as it were, gathering and folding it up like a treasured garment, and putting it away, in the recesses of your mind, for use hereafter. The life and thought and action of you go forward now into the upper portion of the consciousness, and is related to spiritual things more deeply; or, in other words, you have now arrived at that plane of evolution in your spiritual consciousness when you have a higher plane of activities, that, by contrast, because of their refinement, are justly describable as the spiritual plane of your being.

Now this spiritual plane is the complement of the natural plane you existed upon before; it is the very essence of all that has gone before. Whereas love ruled you before, now another power begins to operate as a controlling influence upon your judgment. It is the power of spiritual perception. The spiritual perception operates now, and whereas before you had to reason and to argue upon all that entered into your knowledge, now the soul sees beneath the form, through the phenomenon, to the law and the principle that are beneath it. The more remote powers, as you consider them now, of your souls, are then brought nearer to the surface; and all the virtues and abilities you have dreamed of as being possible hitherto, now become practical realities in your everyday experience.

This spiritual power working within you begins to manifest itself externally, and you behold yourself upon this plane clothed literally in the purity of your own progress; whereas your garments upon the lower or natural plane of spiritual life were the reflection of your personal thoughts and states and conditions, which now have become the outward types and forms of your interior life, and develop a being clothed in

77

that which makes imposition and imposture utterly impossible. Here on this plane of life the spirit always is to outward form just what it is in inward nature. If this sublime law were only realized on earth, what a transformation would be effected in the conditions of human society, how many people would have to change places; those who are up would have to come down, those who are judges would become criminals, while many a poor prisoner might play the role of judge most righteously. Think of it! The time will come when what you really are, out of the purity and sweetness of your progress, will become actually manifest in the external robes that clothe you. This spiritual state brings you into closer sympathy with the souls of men than you could here obtain upon the natural plane previously referred to. Natures intersphere each other more completely, and more close communion exists between the inhabitants of this plane; and their affections and their perceptions, running into closer harmony than hitherto, prevent them making misplaced confidences, wrong associations, and injurious affiliations.

They find, too, that the purposes of being have a deeper significance than they ever dreamed before; and realizing truly and universally the presence of law and principle in the conditions around them and within themselves, they are at last overwhelmed with a deeper and more spiritual consciousness of the existence and the government of God than ever was possible to them before. One step further is taken here; and from this plane of the spiritual perception they arise to still more exalted development, which we will call, for convenience's sake, the Celestial state. There a wondrous development is made manifest; would that we had the power and the skill to bring the glory and the beauty of this third state before your understandings; the radiant divinity of it, the spirit and power, the spirituality of it, the loveliness of it, are so divinely glorious, permeated by such royalty of soul from those who live within it, the omnipotence of God's great presence, that words fall all too short of being able to give you the slightest outline of it.

Lives there beat in glorious rhythm with the eternal music of the Infinite heart itself, and every latent possibility of the soul to this point rises to its highest altitude- manifests its most glorious activities and divinest powers; the noble messengers of that higher life are indeed fitted to be as even gods to you. How can we speak of them, how can we tell you of their glory and their beauty? There is in their natures one great principle. If affection and perception have ruled in the previous cases, now comes the godlike power of meditation, or assimilation, whereby the principles already gathered, the knowledge already possessed, the developments already made manifest, are brought within the very consciousness of the soul itself; and love and intellect and meditation here crown the progress of the soul as it passes upward in the second state. Mark well the meaning of these terms. We are speaking only of the second state- not of other states that rise beyond it, mark you, more glorious still, but that one state of spiritual being that you are at present related to, the three divisions of which we have just enumerated.

When these three separate stages of progress have been made, they may now be passed before you in the review that substantially says they are the fulfillment of the natural man as you know him today. They are the realities of the spiritual man as you feel him within yourselves, they are the blossoming and unfolding of the divine man that lies beneath all that is the very essence of your natures.

Here we have, then, observation, perception, and reflection- love, justice, and wisdom manifesting themselves in their proper orders; and as they increase in power and come into harmony each with the other, and when love is directed by reason, and reason controlled by wisdom, then love, justice, and wisdom- (justice promoting the action of the intellect)- then, when these three are brought into mutual harmony and unity, what a perfectly rounded life, by comparison with the lives of men today, is presented for your consideration!

When this final stage in this second state has been reached, behold! a marvelous thing occurs. The mind's action, or, more correctly speaking, the action of the conscious soul itself, produces a wonderful result; and all that has been so far reached becomes absorbed into the very nature of you, and becomes the foundation element that is the basis of your progress in the next state that rises beyond- the second state you will encounter when you pass from this your first.

The process may be indefinitely repeated. These triune developments, their associations in action and their final assimilation into one compact element, will go on indefinitely; until the soul in its attributes of justice, love, and wisdom, and all the elements that make up man's nature, affectionally, intellectually, and spiritually, shall grow to such gigantic proportions, and possess such divine abilities, that all you have ever dreamed of concerning even Deity himself shall pale into utter insignificance by the side of the reality you shall personally possess. May we not, then, pause here, asking you to remember that we have only dealt in plain and simple terms and on general principles with some of the most important facts which will be your experiences when you pass from this stage to the world beyond? We here endeavor to present to you, not an approximation, but a literal statement of the fact that the three planes of your present natures, the natural, intellectual, and spiritual, as we should, perhaps, more correctly interpret them, are unfolded upon the first general degree of experience after death, and that over there the three are represented by the terms natural, spiritual, and celestial; and as you thus progress, the principles of your divine humanity, the elements of your immortal minds, the qualities of your eternal souls, are successively developed and unfolded as you go along the second plane of your being, and each unfolding lays the possibility of the one that comes afterwards, and, as it grows and develops, it makes you nobler and more divine; until at last, having exhausted the possibilities of the first plane of your spiritual existence, all these beauties and glories in their triune departments become concentrated and embodied in yourself, and behold! a diviner humanity than you ever have dreamed of yet is the glorious and beautiful result.

May we meet you, then, not as dwellers upon the threshold- for then it would pain us to know that you had not yet reached that plane of spiritual development that fitted you to pass behind the outer portals- but let us meet you upon the inner side of the celestial doorway of the two worlds, and grasp your hands, and say we are glad to see you thus unfolded and thus beautified. May this, your plane of natural existence in the spiritual world, lead to that of which we have told you. Then shall we know that you have lived this life worthily, that you have done your best to unfold and exalt your powers and natures, and truly fitted yourselves for that natural, spiritual state that is to be your first experience after death. And, as you march forward, laboring faithfully, earnestly, and zealously, gathering knowledge and increasing in strength and stature, we shall know that you shall surely go forward to that sublime and celestial condition further still. And as you go up there, wise and loving, true and thoughtful, souls will be with you at every point, to give you aid and help whenever you need it.

Live then, in this world, under the solemn and serious consciousness that you are preparing for the second plane of life; and may your deeds and thoughts and growth be such that you shall pass through the Gateway into the natural life that lies beyond, where, under the blessing of the wise and the good, and the Providence of the Eternal Power, you shall learn the mighty lessons of nature as you can never learn them while you are here; for then you shall be able to see beneath the form, beneath the phenomenon, and learn the law and discover the principle of the life and world in which you live.

If thou wilt so live, then you will earn for yourself free admission beyond the threshhold, and hear the glad welcome of the glorious hosts beyond as they speed to meet you and warmly clasp your hands in greeting, 'Welcome! Well done, thou good and faithful worker!'

PRACTICAL OCCULTISM

SIXTH LECTURE

THE SOUL WORLD: ITS HELLS, HEAVENS, AND EVOLUTIONS

Roll aside the curtains of materiality, penetrate through the mists and darkness of ignorance that skirt the passageway between the two worlds, go beyond the doubts and mutations of material thought and enter into the radiant light of the Soul World that lies beyond; and in that fairer country journey with us and to some extent inspect its Hells, its Heavens, and comprehend in some degree the evolutions that are possible there to that life itself as well as to the people who live therein.

This Soul World is the home of arisen humanity, the place where man commences his future of life and conscious existence on what is called the spiritual side of being; where he commences to unfold the latent capacities of his nature to a grander degree than e'er he could while living here below, though before this can be done many things have to be reckoned with. The evils of the past have to be dissipated, superstitions that have accumulated about the person have to be purged from off the nature of the individual; and to accomplish this something of pain and travail must necessarily be endured by all concerned.

It is the greatest mistake to suppose that merely because you enter into the Soul World you are then prepared to receive all wisdom and manifest all excellence. The path of the student is difficult; there is no royal road to knowledge; and whatsoever the soul gains and values the most is always attained with the greatest effort, and sometimes by the deepest suffering. The fires of suffering are among the potent elements that reveal the jewels of your character. So in the Spiritual World it may be, that, in passing through periods of trial and purification, the soul is gradually moving onward to brighter and better things, and gaining in strength and beauty by reason of its suffering.

When at first you enter that soul life, it may seem to you that there is very little difference between that life and the world you have just departed from; to all appearance people will seem much the same to you, the outward circumstances of their lives will have strong marks of similarity, and the general condition of the world itself will be so similar to the general conditions of the world from which you have departed, that you might almost think that you had fallen asleep in one country on the earth, and had awakened in another. Yet this remarkable similarity is a wonderfully beneficent providence upon the part of the Eternal Wisdom; for if the translation from one world to the other involved a sudden and complete change and alteration in conditions and relationships, why then so sudden a change would result in such a shock to the consciousness, that in all probability people would be seriously affected by the suddenness of the transition and its resultant consequences. Divine beneficence thus works to meet the requirements alike of the meanest and the greatest of humanity; for when the average individual awakes and finds himself surrounded with scenes somewhat similar to those with which he has been long acquainted in the world he has left behind, the shock is lessened and he feels how natural it is that he should be living in this new world, and he says, 'It seems to me I have been here before; I am familiar with the scenes and people, and really it is a natural place for me to be;' and there is something of truth in this supposition.

In the hours of sleep, when curtained slumber has enclosed the outward mind and sense, the soul is sometimes awakened to the glories' of the life beyond and has then caught faint glimpses of its beauty, and mingled, perchance, with its people. Therefore when he comes to the Soul World, indistinctly at first, but gradually disclosing itself, he recognizes that the familiarity of the world about him arises from the fact that he has seen and known it before he actually became a permanent resident therein. He enters, then, into a world that is in every way suited by its nature to his needs. At first the character of the change seems but very unimportant- and hence it is that we always say, though sometimes our statement raises some dispute, that from the actual fact of death, in the first instance, there is but little or no change in the character of the individual; but after he has resided in the Soul World for some little time he realizes his condition, and begins to understand that the old standards of determining a man's position do not apply with the same force to his new state. Then he begins to realize that the social life- shall we call it- of the spiritual world rests upon different foundations to those of the social life of the world he has departed from; and instinctively he begins to understand that he will very soon drop into that place or plane or association that his interior spiritual development entitles him to occupy. Then the difficulties of the life begin to assert themselves. What at first seemed plain sailing and easy going; what at first gave him confidence that the wicked were not punished, and made him feel he had cause for secret congratulation; which made him say, 'Ah! you see there is no Hell, no Devil, no vengeful God to punish, no burning lake of fire, there is nothing to fear, as I had been taught;' which causes him for a time to give all his remorse to the winds and made him think he was going to have a 'royal time' over again- presently disappear, and soon some little doubt begins to obtrude itself; a little speck floats across the clear blue of his present pleasure, and he asks himself, 'I don't know; this is curious; what does it mean?'

Ultimately he realizes that this is what it means; that a man is as are his motives; that in the Soul World the order of things is, that, if his secret life be soiled and defiled and he has been living a lie before the world, then, in a very short time, the lie will rise to the surface of his spiritual personality, the deceit will become manifest in his actual appearance, and those who were so glad to see him, and with whom he was so glad to be, will begin to look askance at him, and he will realize that something has gone wrong. He will then learn the lesson, that all association in the spiritual world depends upon the law of mutual affinity and fitness; and if he hath no affinity with and is unfit to mingle with the better sort of those he finds around him, even in the earliest portion of his career, then, most surely, does the law of repulsion begin to exercise its influence, and he is driven out- driven out from those whom he thought he could succeed in blinding as to his real character- driven out from those whom he thought to hoodwink with his pretended and false claims. Repulsion begins to operate between them, and he is bound to go one way, and that way is away from them. Then he begins to understand, that, if there is no Hell and no Devil and no angry Deity to punish him, there is something that exceeds all these three ideas- a something that is working within, a law of repulsion that drives him out, and that entails all the penalties that those triune concepts have previously been associated with; and he begins to wish presently that a Hell and a Devil really did exist- for when a person possessing an undeveloped and abnormally constituted mind and character is driven out to his own society, he begins to realize the fact that his own society is the very worst possible kind of society he can be associated with, and would go anywhere, do anything, frequently, to escape therefrom. Then begins another phase of the problem. He is now getting into Hell!

But the effects of this position vary in almost every case. It may result in the development of rage and hatred, of fierce and bitter strugglings within his own breast- turmoil, passion, and spite in his mind and thought; he will become angry, vengeful, vicious- and every stage in the descending character of these passional developments will be clearly and indelibly marked upon his features and in his character. One point must be here insisted upon. Though these characteristics be expressed in the appearance and personality of the individual, as a rule they are not recognizable to those who live upon the same plane of spiritual unfoldment, nor are they recognizable to any extent by those who are upon a lower plane of development. But they are perfectly plain and easily to be perceived by those who are above them in spiritual development; hence those will see all the peculiarities expressed in the outward and personal characteristics of the individual, and will see that these external manifestations represent the internal conditions; just as among yourselves the expert physiognomist can read in the lineaments and appearance of the face, to a very large extent, the interior character of the individual, so that he makes comparisons between such persons and certain animals that possess certain characteristics- that this man looks like a fox and has a foxy look, and so forth. Now it does not follow that a person has a pig's head, though he has a piggish face. So when you are told that certain spirits have the appearance of foxes and other animals you may take it that such appearances are but symbolical presentations; and the spirit who is making the statement to the foregoing effect does so sincerely, no doubt, through not having a clear conception of the law in the matter just alluded to.

Whereas you should understand all that is really implied is an indication of the still-continued undevelopment of the spirits thus described. Now these people we are referring to descent into Hell. They may become vengeful, moody, or active; they may brood in silence and secrecy, or they may join others like themselves; for they carry forward the dispositions they possessed while living in this world, and you may find them quarreling while among themselves as they did here below.

This interpretation of their characters gives you the keynote to their personal dispositions. In brief, we may say that all those who are in Hell are those souls that are living disorderly lives. A disorderly life is one that is out of direct relationship with the external laws of progress and development, for by this progress and development you insure true unfolding, and its consequent of happiness.

Disorder, then, is the key-note of the hellish and of the hell world, and this disorder brings us now to the task of locating the exact place where it is. It is not in cavernous recesses where murky clouds lower, and there are burning and roiling waves of fire and flame, away from the light and the glory of the day-deep bosomed in the very bowels of nature herself, where demons gnash their teeth and hurl their anathemas against the goodness of God. God never made such hells as these. He had no necessity to do so; for the hells of the spiritual world are within the individuals who are experiencing the results of all the conditions their actions can create. A disorderly individual having disorder in himself (using the term in the higher spiritual sense) has hell within him. As the old teaching has told you very truly that the Kingdom of Heaven is within you, so also may its opposite be within you; and this being true, Hell being within the disorderly life of the disorderly liver, that Hell can never be escaped from until those who dwell within the sphere of its influence themselves unlock and unbolt the bars of their disorderly living and emerge into the heavens that lie beyond. Hell, then, is purely a personal question, and individual experiences will vary in their intensity and character in accordance with the circumstances of the particular person concerned.

Thus, you will understand, that no actual theological Hell can be found in the Soul World,, but, instead, that each one makes his own Hell- and making it himself he cannot complain against the Almighty Providence for giving him too much, for he creates all he experiences; thus every cause for complaint of injustice is destroyed. Dealing with the matter in this light, we have dealt with it only in its personal application. Let us direct your attention now to some of the hells that literally exist in actual outward form in the Soul World. This seeming contradiction will explain itself in a moment or two. You look with us, standing by our side, and with astonishment you say:

"This cannot be Hell. See those towering mountains that rear their purple domes into the azure hues beyond. See those glowing colors that bathe the whole scene in radiant beauty. Behold those magnificent flowers, those graceful trees, those streams like silver threads winding among the green grasses that wave and roll on their pleasant banks. See those charming lakes- surely these are not the adjuncts of Hell? And those noble edifices lifting their symmetrical domes heavenward; those stately men and women, those youths and maidens, those children- they are not devils living in Hell. Why, how can you call this Hell? How can you say these are devils? There must be something wrong here. The picture is too fair and lovely in its character. Surely you must be wrong?"

No, we are not wrong; all this is- can be seen by you there. But question one of these inhabitants and ask him what he sees. You observe the lines of care upon his brow; he is sad, subdued, and sullen; there is a terrible look lurking in his eye, and latent anger seems to be slumbering within. 'Oh, this place is a horrible place' he answers. 'See those towering walls bleak and dark as the eternal granite. Look at these stagnant streams; they stink in one's nostrils; the air is full of vile odors; the very trees are stripped and bare, there are no blossoms. Look at these people; they are hateful and I loathe their presence. Oh, if I could only get away from here, and be free again, how happy I should be!'

What is the cause of the obliquity of vision which so changes all these transcendent glories we described a moment since? The difference is this: You looked through eyes unclouded; you looked through your better thought and nature; while he sees but through his own disordered and demoralized thought and feeling. The fairest flowers do not attract his gaze, the verdant hills and luxuriant valleys are bare and barren, the trees are stark and naked, the musical and crystal streams are but turbid waters. When the mind is unattuned to the beauty and glory of nature and the harmonies of God, then all of being is bare and bleak and dreadful, and your fellow creatures seem like foes and vile. People in this condition are mentally and spiritually demoralized for the time being, out of order with nature, and out of relationship with God; or, as you would say, psychologically insane, and see existence not as it is, but in the light of their own perverted states. Reflection, however, at last penetrates through the obscuring mists of their disordered minds.

Why are they here? If the spiritual life is a natural life, if the Soul World is for every one and all, why do they come here? they ask themselves. The answer is that they are brought there unknowing to themselves by a power superior to their own, and being there are literally held there. How so? Some things in the spirit-world are done much better than they are done among yourselves, and this is one of them. Sometimes the absurd idea of the liberty of the individual is carried to too great a length among yourselves, and results most disastrously; for it is not right that the untrained and the ignorant and the vicious should have the same absolute liberty and freedom in the community in which they move as the virtuous and the good. This is a problem we suggest to you for your own consideration. You have to protect yourselves against them; and that protection carried one step further might restrain within well-defined limits, and make you realize the fact that those out of relationship with the best conditions, and the best form of human society, should be legitimately restrained by those wiser and better than themselves. In this very Hell we are speaking of this law holds good.

PRACTICAL OCCULTISM

The wise and philanthropic spirits, the great and the good, through all their tributary and subordinate agencies, exercise control. They bring in, from time to time, men and women, youths and maidens, within whom they see the possible development, this sprouting to life, so to speak, of their several natures- they are brought within the magic circle, shall we say, within the spiritual sphere belonging to this locality- and the general influence of the protecting minds makes a wall around this place that these feebler wills are utterly incapable of passing through. They meet a barrier; what it is they cannot tell, but they are conscious of a superior force, the character of which they cannot define.

There they are kept until this sphere of influence gradually penetrates their thoughts and infuses itself into their minds, stimulates their moral character and quality, and develops their latent possibilities into action. Then, as the mind becomes orderly, as the soul comes into right relationship with the spiritual surroundings that belong to it, in the place where they are, behold, they begin to see the sunshine; blades of green grass begin to take the place of barren soil they have seen so long; the very trees begin to put forth their leaves again, and the turbid waters seem to move with a quicker motion. Little by little the beauty of the scene begins to unfold itself. You may take it from us, that the more of beauty you can see in your external surroundings, the more of beauty is there developed within yourself. So as these disorderly minds become adjusted and reduced to due relationship, to the conditions with which they are surrounded, behold their mental and moral natures begin to assert themselves, and their intuitions and aspirations begin to make music in their happy souls; little by little they begin to realize that the Hell in which they lived was a great Sanitarium, a great Health College, where under salutary moral influences they have been gradually brought out of the Hell that the disorderly conditions of their past life created within themselves.

PRACTICAL OCCULTISM

Thus the hells of the Soul World are educational, reformatory, spiritually and morally hygienic, so to speak. Those only are brought into them in whom it is seen the harmonies and germs of goodness are beginning to sprout; and these being thus treated are by degrees brought into active relationship with those who instruct and surround them, their special adaptations and qualifications are discovered, and they are in time transferred to other educational places, where these qualities can be nourished and developed into health and activity. Thus from the lowest hells spring forth the angels we shall deal with next. Before leaving the hells and their inhabitants there is another peculiar point we would like to impress upon you which concerns the souls living therein, for in many cases they appear to grow worse after they have passed into the spiritual world. You must remember that there is in every one of you a certain amount of disorder, disease of body, obliquity of mind, and perversion of moral consciousness,- all of which are potent elements of evil and wrong-doing. If you cannot exhaust the germs of these things while you are living in this world, if they are not expelled by the superior moral faculties and intellectual and spiritual development while here on earth, then will they cling to your mental sphere and effect their out-working when you get into the spiritual world. Do not, though, for one instant construe th argument that every man has so much wickedness, therefore he has got to be wicked to get rid of it, and thereby excuse the wickedness of yourself or your neighbor. Nothing of the sort is here involved. There is this possible misdirection in you all, but its true and legitimate expulsion is through developing more and more of the spiritual attributes, which is your duty here. If you do not get rid of this possible element of degradation while here, then it will have to exhaust itself in the spiritual world; and apparently it will result in your becoming much worse after death than before.

The end comes at last; the period of reaction asserts

itself. At such times some gentle brother, from one of the great benevolent Brotherhoods who have charge of these hells we have just mentioned, is able to take you, unconsciously to yourself, and place you in one of the Sanitariums we have portrayed, and in the end effect your purification.

But come with us to fairer scenes, if possible; though surely we may say this scene is fair enough- for wherever the doing of good to your fellows is involved, there shall we find beauty and sweetness, and something akin to the beneficence and love of God himself is there. We come, then, to what, for convenience' sake, we will call the fairer scenes of the soul World, where the souls of men are supposed to be basking in everlasting felicity, where eternal sunshine reigns supreme, where happiness, pleasure, and joy are perpetual. 'Yes,' you will say, 'one would like to find that such things were true, one would very like to discover such things after death; if we could only enter there and enjoy all the beatitudes of such a condition, how happy should we be for the change!' At first you will not find such things; the everlasting and eternal sunshine is a dream that we do not think you will realize for ages yet to come; the alternations of joy and sorrow, of shade and sunshine, of hope and fear, of success and failure, are necessities to the immortal soul for ages yet to be- and in these heavens there will be no one uninterrupted and glowing day, no unceasing tide of joy, no unvarying sunshine; the soul has to grow, man has to advance step by step and gain experience; experience brings him knowledge. But while he is gathering knowledge through experience, failures and disasters are sure to assail his progress from time to time.

Therefore the heavens will not be altogether devoid of their cares and anxieties, shall we call them, not altogether devoid of their aspects of gloom; and yet because of the germs of sweetness and order and beauty belonging to them, it shall make these as fleeting shadows, passing across the path of human life-only as a fitful cloud briefly shutting out the golden sunlight.

'What shall we find in those heavens?' What do we mean by Heaven? As Hell is within, so also is Heaven. It is no more a locality than Hell. The sense of order, peace, and righteousness, consequent upon well doing, within the breast, makes the place a Heaven; and in the Societies, Fraternities, Families, and Associations of the Soul World the pure soul lives in sweetest bonds of unity. There in that happy estate you shall find all that the souls of men desire- all their hopes realized, all their affections ministered to, all their aspirations unfolded to the point that they have reached.

What shall be the evolutions that arise from the heavens and the hells we have just referred to? For one might truly say that the heavens are the evolution of the hells; indeed, when we take life right through, in every case do we find that each ascending stage is an evolution from the stage that preceded it. What then is beyond these heavens? When the minds and souls of men grow strong enough they plume themselves for flight to higher regions, and all the conditions of disorder and inharmony disappear from the realms belonging to their existence on the planes described; all shall then be order, harmony, and peace-and on the particular plane of spiritual existence we have been detailing, there shall be embodied within yourselves all the latent possibilities that will then have become actualities. Then, the essential principles being thus embodied within the consciousness of those who live upon that plane of life, behold the old heavens shall be rolled away as a scroll, so to speak, and those who have lived therein go to higher states still; where still nobler elements of spiritual life shall be evolved- where what you have reasoned upon, what you have thought upon, and experimented upon, in preceding stages, shall then become actual and positive knowledge that shall be as plain and clear to you as the simplest of simple things among yourselves today.

Then shall the soul unfold new powers, new qualities and orders of action- new and stronger associations shall arise, and over all shall brood the consciousness that there is a mightier than thou, a deeper than that which hath yet been revealed or done, a grander than even you have yet dreamed of; and your search for the mystic words of wisdom, your desire to find the deeper fountain yet undiscovered, shall bubble up with renewed force and power within your souls whenever you but do and dare for the greater truths as you did and dared for the radiance and glory of that Heaven you have now attained. Then shall all feuds be stayed, all hatreds of the mind be quenched, all the discords of affection be stilled, all the differences and dissensions that ever keep the human lives and loves apart be banished forever; and the great family of humanity shall become one spiritual brotherhood of happy and united souls in the more real Soul World that lies far, far beyond the conditions of the Soul World that we have just been dealing with.

Thus, briefly, we have endeavored to place before you the quality and character of the hells and the heavens, and the evolution of possible greatness and grandeur in yourselves, in the conditions of being that will meet you after you master the first conditions of the Soul World into which you enter immediately following your departure from physical existence here.

Thus discord and harmony, as you will have learned, are the key-notes of the hells and heavens of spiritual existence; and the lesson we wish to enforce clearly upon you is, that the Divine Providence has not made one condition or state bleak and barren and wretched and miserable for those who are unhappy and in darkness and misery, and another condition of divine beauty and glory for those who are morally and spiritually progressed; but that the Soul World, like the Natural World, is a bright and beautiful world in every department, and that you see and interpret its character through the medium of the discord or harmony that resides within your own breast and is manifested in your own mind. Take this lesson to your heart, and then you will realize that as is your own character and development, so will be your interpretation of the condition of existence in which you happen to be situated. Now, let us withdraw you from this fair world to the realms of mortal being again, leaving its glory and its beauty as a memory bright and pleasant to linger within your thoughts- coming down from these Brotherhoods, these Families and Fraternities, from these noble and philanthropic hearts, so that you may again be practical dwellers in mortal life; and as the curtains roll behind you, as you retire from the glory that lies behind them and again tread the terrestrial fields, oh! remember but a thin veil hangs between yourselves and that world from which in mind you have now returned; that, if you wish to enter into the calmer heavens over there, see that heavenly conditions are unfolded within your lives and breasts while here on earth. Remember also that surely you shall find an entrance into the hells that lie beyond, as a consequence of the discords in your natures now. Strive, then, to reduce all discords to harmony- purify yourselves from all unclean thoughts, desires, and deeds- lift your natures up to the highest plane of personal application, morally and spiritually; live so purely before the world that, like the brightest silver, if but a breath rests upon it, it vanishes ere the stain can fairly be said to have been seen. Keep your hearts so purged, your souls so pure and sweet, that no stain can ever rest upon them; and when you die, when you pass through the mystic portals into the Soul World beyond, then shall you be fitted to enter into some of its heavenly associations by having a heavenly condition already developed within yourselves- and that shall measurably assist you to come under the influence of that greater and grander evolution that we have suggested as possible for the inhabitants of the Soul World beyond.

PRACTICAL OCCULTISM

SEVENTH LECTURE

LIFE, DEVELOPMENT, AND DEATH IN SPIRIT-LAND

When you remember that life for the inhabitants of the spirit-land means an eternity of life, and that the argument is an unending existence, you may naturally inquire, Is it possible that the bodies of the people living in the immortal world shall continue to maintain their structure and their functions for such an enormous duration? There is, of course, to the majority of people living on the mortal plane, the idea of friction, waste, and consequent decay, as being facts they are familiar with in association with material bodies- and it will be urged that if there are functions and activities associated with the spiritual bodies there must necessarily be friction, waste, and decay in connection with those bodies; and while people may, in a certain sense, be able to grasp the conception of the eternal duration of those bodies, they certainly are unable, in the great majority of cases, to dispense with the supposition of friction, waste, and decay, as previously stated. That these are factors in all organic structures on the mortal plane is self-evident. Have they to be considered in regard to the organic structures of the spiritual plane? and if so, what are the means whereby that waste is repaired, and that friction reduced to the lowest minimum? These are deep questions, and asked in vain of the usual and accepted authorities upon such subjects.

Now the development of the spiritual personality in the spirit-life is also another important question; for if there be a development there must either be an expansion of existing materials or an aggregation thereto- for the development must either proceed from within or be the consequence of additions from without. It matters little whether it be development of soul or mind or body, the law must hold good in either case- and if one case, in all cases; and the solution will have to be sought as to where is the source of the means of the possible development of the individual inhabitant of the spiritual world.

We will also, as another interesting speculation, ask the question, If the duration of the personal existence in the spiritual world is eternal, and the development of the individual is eternal also, may there not come a time when the personality of the individual will have grown so enormous in proportions as to be practically unwieldly? When we introduce the speculation we have to deal with, the possibility of death in the spiritual world, a wave of fear and sadness may, as it were, roll over your spirits- a chilling blast may seem to sweep across the eager buds of your aspiring natures; and you may say, if we have to face the grim monster again after passing through mortal death, then the exchange has advantaged us but little! Yet having realized that death in your mortal conditions is only a stepping-stone to a larger life, and having gained the confidence of victory in one case, the assurance of victory in all cases where a like experience is to be encountered may almost be counted upon as certain. If existence in the higher life leads you to higher powers and the exercise of greater ability, it follows that every seeming obstacle in your path will grow less powerful the more exalted you become yourselves.

Life in the spirit-land means several things as associated with the individual. It means spiritual life, mental life, personal life; for you must bear in mind that the inhabitants of the spiritual world are just as much beings, persons, men and women, as are yourselves; that they are endowed with the machinery for the expression of intelligence, just the same as humanity; that they, any more than yourselves, have not yet reached a plane where they are able to express intelligence apart from organization. Now this is a most important fact to be considered. You must bear in mind that in all cases the exhibition of force is dependent upon an agency for a manifestation. It matters not what the ultimate expression may be, the agency is the thing contended for; and as intelligence, as a force in man's personal nature, is dependent upon an agency for its expression, you must have in spirit-land, as here, an organization- and this organization is the agency for the expression of your intelligence, and the manifestations of the inherent powers of your immortal entity.

Then the existence of this organization, the reparation of its waste, the reduction of the results of its friction to its lowest possible minimum, are questions fairly and legitimately before us for consideration. Here it follows that the spirit-body being upon a higher plane than the mortal body, its [functional operations will involve another set of laws, and those laws will be upon the higher plane, as is the body they are associated with; and whereas there are certain processes that are absolutely necessary in the material life, their counterparts may be accomplished by other methods and higher laws than those by which they are accomplished while you are living here on earth. The processes of physical existence may be thus summarized:

You consume food; the heat and chemical action in the various organs of digestion reduce the food to its component elements, which elements are distributed to the various portions of the system. Through the various activities there is a waste of tissue, and this expenditure is repaired by the liberation of the essential elements or forces of the foods or substances which, being absorbed into the human organism, sustain and repair it. Therefore, ultimately, it is the forces of nature that sustain the human organism; and the process whereby you reach these forces is the process of destructive assimilation, as expressed in the digestion of human food. This is apparently a roundabout process, you will say. It is particularly fit and proper for the plane of life upon which it operates, and it would be improper and inadequate and utterly unfit if applied to beings living upon a higher plane than that you at present occupy. But if the question of assimilated forces on the lower plane has to receive attention, why should not also be considered the assimilation of forces upon the higher plane ? If the elaboration and absorption of forces is the means whereby reparation is accomplished here, may it not also be that upon the higher plane a similar process is also involved? And if so, shall it not be further accepted that the means whereby this result is obtained upon the higher plane shall be a higher method, as compared with the method you depend upon in this world? If we accept the position that the organization of the spirit-body and its processes are to a certain extent a duplicate of the material organization, then the question becomes a point of interest as to what use the duplicates of the great organs of the interior of the system are subservient, what are their counterparts in the spiritual personality, and how are their functions accomplished there. If we take the duplication of the organism as a spiritual fact, and that it contains within itself the spiritual counterparts of most of the organs you are familiar with in the human physiology, then we have to assure you that that internal organism becomes, as it were, a species of battery, a collection of cells or sacs- whereby in the peculiar structure and formation of the spirit body the essential forces of the spiritual realm are extracted, and are sent on their mission for absorption into, and the consequent maintenance of, ethereal organizations that constitute your bodies there; that instead of the grosser fluids of the material organization, the etherealized electricities and magnetisms of the spiritual world are the circulating mediums in the spirit organization.

Now the operations of the spiritual physiology, shall we call it, to use a term to convey the idea clearly to you, necessarily involve the expenditure of force, just the same as the operations of your earthly body, when, having exhausted its forces in the accomplishment of any particular object, they have to be recruited and restored by means of the forces elaborated and distilled by the digestive and assimilating agencies of the system from the food consumed; so in the spirit body, corresponding processes are necessary to distill the elements and forces that are needed to establish and maintain health and action in the spirit beings. Now this necessarily demands not only the expenditure of force, but may possibly involve the expenditure of substance as well, and this substance has to be again supplied; for the structure has to be continually built up and sustained, as well as its depleted forces restored- which, when the needful processes are duly fulfilled, is satisfactorily accomplished and the structure sustained.

Therefore the life of the individual in the spirit-land is sustained by these electrical and magnetic processes and distillations in a manner somewhat analogous to, though not exactly the same as, the means depended upon on the grosser plane. We might, in a word, sum the argument up by saying, that the processes of material existence are the prophecy, dim, faint, and indistinct, of the higher laws and methods whereby life is sustained in the spirit-land. A little experiment, which will at once assure you of the fact that it is possible to sustain life by principle of absorption, consists in the immersion of a portion of the physical body in water; the system will absorb the water- a certain action called endosmose, which the scientific mind is familiar with, will enable the structure to absorb the water, enabling the person to thus obtain whatever nourishment the system needs. You may try the experiment for yourself; if you are suffering from excessive thirst and heat, place your hand underneath the water faucet, and gradually a cool influence will spread through the entire body as the water flows over your hand. The coolness and absorbed moisture will gradually spread throughout the entire system, restoring the lacking fluid that causes you to experience the thirst. Now this is a very simple fact, but it contains a deep prophecy of the law of absorption as one of the means of subsistence in the spiritual life. Magnetically or psychologically the same law is operating. You absorb one another's influences, you absorb each other's affections and hatreds, each other's health and disease. Constantly and continually you are subject to this law of absorption; and when you see that this law is but the prophecy of its operation upon a higher plane and under better circumstances, you can understand that our argument is not strange or far-fetched.

Here, then, we have found something of the means of life for the people living in the spiritual world, and we find that life is active and operative there, as it is among yourselves, and the men and women there have a reality pertaining to their natures that has not often been supposed- that ignorance, fanaticism, and superstition unfortunately have hitherto entirely denied; that the problem of subsistence of life in the spiritual world has been altogether ignored in the spiritual training the world has received in former times; and that subsistence there follows at first certain general lines of similarity with this life, but that ultimately the law of subsistence by absorption is the rule in the higher spiritual states. Coming to the matter of Development in the spiritual world we have to consider two questions: development as applied to the personality of the individual, and development as applied to his individuality and consciousness, if we may be permitted to use familiar terms as applied to the outer and inner nature of the people of the spirit-life.

The objective, or, more correctly, the organic, part of the spirit has an eternal persistence of duration; if the form is eternal, and the development of it is eternal, you might ask if the individual would not at last gross so unwieldy in proportion as to be utterly incapable of locomotion. This is not true. So far as we have been able to trace the law, it is impossible for the personal development of the individual to ever attain such enormous proportions as to utterly deprive him of the power of using his body in any sense whatever- the reason of which we will show you presently.

Now the mental and spiritual development of the individual runs on indefinitely, but you must remember that mental growth and spiritual growth in all cases depend upon self-effort; there is no growth without work, that is to be distinctly borne in mind. You can starve your mind and soul just as truly as you may your body; and if you will not pluck from the trees of truth in the vales of wisdom, you certainly will not grow in mind, any more than you would grow in stature if you were to refuse to eat the necessary articles of subsistence in the material life. In the spiritual life you must work for mental growth and spiritual development, and unless you do so work you will not gain either. This work must be intelligent work; for as you starve your bodies by eating improper food, so, mentally, you may starve your mind by improperly feeding it, and to such an extent that mental digestion is arrested- and then the mind will be surely starved, as would the body under similar circumstances. Your work must be within the limitation of your present abilities; and as you consume your ability, so to speak, in an intelligent effort, thus you build up your mental characters and nature. Fill up and grow sturdy in your minds, and your increase of strength and knowledge will enable you to deal with still greater problem- the mastering of which will give you strength and stature in mind as a consequence of knowledge gained.

Spiritual unfoldment is apt to be considered as the great thing all should strive for. There is a sort of idea among many people, a loose and indistinct idea it seems to us, that spiritual development is the only development worth having. In the name of common sense what do you mean by spiritual development? Do not all the forces of mind, affection, and every intellectual quality and character of your nature, all the forces and expressions of your conscious life, proceed from your immortal entity?

Some people seem to think that spirituality is a sort of golden cake that they may take a bite out of and be benefited, the same as the eating of manna in the olden times. Nothing of the sort. The spirituality of the individual does not depend upon the cultivation of one special department, but upon the entire rounding out of the whole nature, mentally, morally, and spiritually; and when this development of character is strong, the individual, self-poised and self-centered, can rise triumphant over the ills of time, over the evils of the flesh, over the perplexities of daily life- ride the storms of hatred in safety and security, and emerge at last into the clear waters of a conscious self-poised existence, fearing no sorrow and dreading no future; then there is a spiritual development worthy of the name, made up of the personal, mental, moral, and conscious development of the individual who is concerned.

But such lives have neither time nor inclination to mourn, cry, or yearn for an especial spiritual development; for they feel the spirituality of their own souls radiating to every department of their being, and expressed in every thought and action of their lives. This is the spiritual development we would suggest to you as being realized in the spirit-life. Over there it is not the question of the development of one especial part of a person's nature to make them prominent or noticeable, or to give them some especial grace and quality. He is considered the most spiritual who has the most of spirituality in the entirety of his life, character, thought, and action. Hence, then, in the spirit-land, the question of development may be followed upon any particular plane that you please. One person may make an especial point of development in a certain direction, another person's inclination running in some other channel may cause him to pursue development in some opposite direction; yet you could not accuse either of being non-spiritual,for they are pursuing whatever way, that, to their necessities and consciousness, seems the correct and proper way for them to pursue; and for them it is, because it seems so to them. When you can convince them that it is not the proper way and cause their thoughts to flow into other channels, then the new way will be the proper one for them. The development in the spiritual world may be intellectual, moral, or spiritual; it may be aesthetic, artistic, poetic, affectional; it may be the hundred and one different things by which the mind and soul and consciousness round out in so many departments, in the many different methods of progress and unfolding; but whatever way the line of progress may be pursued, the development comes as the natural consequence of the result of intelligent labor wisely directed.

What is the consequence of this development ? This development of power supposes the development of the means for the utilization of power. The development of faculties, and the development of functions, must proceed side by side with development of organic means of expression. Now, in the spirit-life, the means of expression that are depended upon, in the earlier stages at least, are the means which are the subjective means to you in this world; and the subjective powers of your present nature become the objective features of expression in your early conditions in the spirit-state.

The result of this is, that there is not only an acquisition of power immediately upon entering the spiritual world, but there is a further development of that power as a consequence of life and action on that plane; remembering now that for every being there is a development of ability, there must be a development of means through which that ability is acquired and expressed- that is, the organic means by which knowledge is gained implies another set of means whereby knowledge, after it is gained, can be put into practical operation. The spiritual brain, the spiritual sensibilities, the spiritual activities, the spiritual agencies, or senses shall we call them, that you utilize in the spiritual world for the acquisition of knowledge, have still a subjective side- which is affected by the knowledge when gained, and enables it to be expressed after you have mastered it and made it part and parcel of your own experiences.

But why is it impossible that the development and life of the individual can never become so enormous as to become unwieldy, as we have suggested? This brings us to the question we have to deal with next- death in the spirit-land. If there is a process of expansion in the personality, the consciousness, and mentality of the spirit, there is a process of precipitation and concentration also. You continually grow in knowledge, your mind expands, and it contains so many things that you begin to feel the necessity of setting your mental house in order. What illustration can we give you? Here is a merchant: business pours in upon him thick and fast, he has a large correspondence from all quarters of the globe; there he sits at his desk, around him are pigeon-holes without number, where in proper order he puts his various correspondence, letters, and bills, and notices that come before him. But his papers have accumulated to such an extent that he says, 'Dear me, I am getting overwhelmed with papers and documents- what shall I do with them?' Then he thinks he will have them all gone through; and those that are useless and out of date he will destroy, and those that are of some service he will enter on the pages of a book conveniently arranged for that purpose.

Then the process of precipitation and concentration begins; a portion of the papers are noted by a few lines in the book, and either filed away or perchance destroyed. The more important are carefully reduced to small bundles and stored away in the cellar, in case there may be occasion to refer to them in the future. By these methods many a pigeon-hole is cleared entirely, and the contents of others are materially reduced; so that the merchant says at the end of the clearing up, 'Now I have got all of the important matters in this book properly indexed, where I can make ready reference to bygone transactions, and have plenty of room for the new correspondence.' He has concentrated and precipitated the experiences of the past year, he has reduced them to small dimensions; and his old correspondence not being allowed to remain in an unwieldy condition, he now can dispose of his new correspondence with ease, and handle it without difficulty.

In the spiritual world you will ultimately find yourself in a condition similar to that of the merchant. Your mind will be stored with memorandums of investigation of a thousand different things, and you will begin to realize that you are becoming overburdened. Then you will pass your mental treasures in review, and finding certain things not altogether necessary for your well-being, they may well be put away. And little by little you gradually go through your whole account of mental treasures, and reduce them to the smallest possible compass; and the mind's actions being thus reduced and concentrated, the volume of preceding experiences that are in the memory will be reduced to the narrowest compass- and you will be thus able to start again with more room in the memory, more room in the drawers of your mind, ready for larger things hereafter.

But this process cannot be fully accomplished without a certain peculiar condition, and here we shall have to digress a moment or two to introduce a point of spiritual philosophy that we think is well worthy of your consideration. The three-fold operations of the mind may be described as perception, observation, and reflection. This leads to the process of assimilation as the result of the three processes referred to; and the mind, assimilating the products obtained by one or all of these three processes, unites in a concrete whole the materials thus acquired.

Now the three planes of mental and spiritual action are love, justice, and wisdom, corresponding to the physical or natural, the mental, and spiritual natures of the individual. Now, when you are living in this world, you are living altogether upon the physical plane of existence; and when you die here, the essence of all the experiences you have passed through are concentrated in your memory at the time of your passage from one world to the other. Also, when you pass from one plane to the other of spiritual existence, a process somewhat similar and analogous to that passed through upon passing from this stage to the next beyond it has to be encountered; and the result is a concentration of all the experiences and results upon that spiritual plane, so that you consolidate the experiences of that plane of being, and they become the foundation of your mental being when you arrive on the plane above.

How, then, do you die in the spiritual world? Have you to be sick? Oh, no! You will please bear in mind that in this matter we are speaking of your translation from one of the grand planes of spirit life to another- not of a mere change of sphere, society, or association, but of an absolute removal from one condition of spiritual existence to another that lies beyond it. You are not sick, there is no disease, no illness; but yet you are about to be translated from one condition of life to another beyond it. Are you fitted for it? Yes, you have been growing towards it; your spiritual perceptions have been quickened, and you see clearly there is a higher realm beyond you than the one you are at present residing in, and you realize it is a state that you have to enter. How can you gain admission? There comes a time when that plane of spiritual life that you are now on has been exhausted- an indefinite age may pass before such a result is attained, but come that time surely will and does- and then there is this process of assimilation we have previously referred to. Thoughts, as it were, concentrate; you feel a nameless but sweet and beautiful rest stealing over you; you feel that you are going to vastate the cruder elements of the condition you are then in. A beautiful sleep will fall upon you, and while this sleep is on you, behold! these elements will drop from you, as the dew may fall from the tree. You awake presently, and in that waking find that you have made the voyage from the state you were then in to the wonderful clime you now have reached. No pain, no sorrow- scarcely a change in form even; but certain grosser spiritual elements, that were fit and proper to the condition before, have been left behind.

And when, with a greater activity of the powers of your immortal nature, you stand on the higher plane, the whole of your preceding life is there enshrined within your mental nature, spread out before your mind's eye, whensoever you choose to view them; and profiting by what you have obtained before, realizing it is but the stepping-stone to what now lies before you, you will then start upon the new career that there awaits you.

This may involve a separation of greater or less duration from those whom you have been previously associated with. If you have attained a higher plane of spiritual existence, you will have to wait until your friends have reached the same development ere they can stand side by side with you in the same condition of spiritual unfolding. Here we have, then, in brief review, passed before you the questions of Life and Development and Death in spirit land. Let us look at the matter of death, however, from another point of view- which does not mean translation from one stage to another in the meaning in which we have just placed it before you. There are many who have to die from old prejudices, from old affections and old loves; many who have to die morally and mentally ere they can be resurrected from the crudities and imperfections and errors and mistakes that have accumulated while here below. This accumulation will have to be vastated, thrown off- the old will have to die, and the new man come to life. Many and many such a death have we witnessed in the spiritual world: you say here it is repentance; we see it over and over again a thousand different times.

Die to the old and live to the new; die to the false and live to the true; and by so 'dying' and so 'coming to life' you can attain a freedom and beauty, and an impetus of development, that cannot come to you by any other means. There are hatreds that will have to die before love can bloom; there is ignorance that must die ere wisdom can take its place; there is the calloused cold-heartedness that must die ere the warm, rich life of love can animate the soul itself; there are all these influences and associations to die from ere the jewels of character and the beauties of the inner life can fill your mind.

In thus placing before you Life, Development, and Death in spirit-land, we trust you will agree that we have given you some clear and precise information upon the various topics considered. Our object and desire has been to do this, so that you may learn in some degree what are the actual facts of man's post-mortem life and character.

PRACTICAL OCCULTISM

APPENDIX: ANSWERS TO QUESTIONS - REMARKS BY THE CONTROL

We have now reached that stage in our labors with you. the present Class, at which we shall be enabled to consider any questions you may desire to propound to us, and help you to remove any difficulties or doubts that may linger in your minds concerning any of the matters we have touched upon during this course of lessons. Our desire is to assist you to the very best of our ability in any direction that you may require aid. Of course we do not claim that we have entirely exhausted the various subjects we have dealt with ; in many cases we have only been able to be suggestive, and point, rather, to the much more that remained behind than to ask you to accept as complete the little that we have been able to present. You understand us well enough by this time to know that we have no desire to dogmatize, or to demand that you accept what we say simply because we say it. In the agitation of thought is the beginning of wisdom; in mutual counsel there lies safety; and in the free, frank, and honest discussion of all difficulties there lies the only salvation from ignorance and superstition.

Q. What is the distinction between the will of the individual and the mind?

A. The will is the executive officer of the mind under the direct control of the consciousness. The mind is largely memorative and cognitive- is engaged in the acquisition of external facts. The inner side of the mind is, of course, related to the consciousness; and the exhibition of energy from the essential soul, the conscious me, as represented in what is called the will, intelligently directs the mental machinery for the accomplishment of specific ends and purposes. The distinction between the will and the mind is so exceedingly subtle that it is

111

very difficult to express it in precise and definite terms, so that it may be easily apprehended. But what we have said, we think, may help you to understand the lines of distinction between them. The will is the executive officer of the consciousness working through the mind.

Q. In higher realms do not family ties become swallowed up in a great and universal love for all?

A. In the more advanced realms of spiritual existence, such is the case; and the love of the family association as a unit, the parental, selfish enjoyment, is expanded to a larger and broader life and character.

This much should be borne in mind: that love which is purely local and domestic has within itself the germ, the essential element, of an enduring relation; and that enduring relation blossoms,expands,and beautifies, and is not destroyed- and this is embodied and included within the boundaries of the larger love for the human race at large. Though the larger then contains the lesser, the lesser is not destroyed altogether in its character by its expansion and association with the larger. Those who are truly related spiritually, those whose lives are entwined together by interior powers and bonds, remain in such relationship, in such unity and such affection indefinitely; but their ideas broaden out, their perception increases in various directions, and their operations extend over a wider area.

So long as love is a personal, individual, and local question, you have only reaped one-half of its benefits; but when it brings you out into a wider sphere of operation, and you begin to have a love for humanity, the individual is then elevated into a broader sphere of life and progress.

PRACTICAL OCCULTISM

Q. Are there not those in celestial spheres who have no anxiety, fear,or doubt, and who know the exact result of any work they undertake?

A. On the plane of their own development it is perfectly correct to say that they are without fear or doubt as to the result of any work they undertake; because they have within themselves, within their mental and personal view and understanding, the laws and principles of the results that are to be accomplished. But when they aim to accomplish something which is beyond them, which leads them into unfamiliar grounds, then, like yourselves, the element of uncertainty enters into their calculations, and they may require assistance and advice from others. In the accomplishment of labor upon planes of operation beneath them, there is less hesitancy or doubt than would be supposed to be the case upon their own especial plane of development; for having mastered all beneath them, and having had practical experience on those lower planes, they know exactly when to do their work and how to do it- just as a mathematician is certain that he can accomplish certain results in the use of figures, because he has all its laws and principles at his fingers' ends. But when he attempts to work in new and unfamiliar fields, then experiments have to be made; and they are the subjects of doubt and uncertainty, because of lack of familiarity with the means to be employed to reach the desired end. Thus it is there is no royal road to absolute knowledge, save that royal road all have to tread- the road of personal effort, and individual activity. So far as you have gone you are a master, and you are a master indeed if you are able to comprehend that which surrounds you in your then present condition. But when you go beyond it you have to make effort again, individual activity is again called for, and you have to work up to the higher grades beyond you, even as you have had to work from the lower grade you have emerged from and ascended out of.

PRACTICAL OCCULTISM

Q. How can a developed medium know whether it will be beneficial or injurious to yield to spirit influence?

A. The most practical way of deciding the question is to decide by the results of experience. You cannot decide until results are presented, and in this, experience, great care, and thoughtfulness should be used. A temporary inconvenience, and distress or disturbance, should not be confounded with the possibility of perpetual disturbance and continued distress. When mediumship develops in the individual there is, so to speak, a sort of interruption of the psychical and mental currents of the life, and consequent disturbance in almost every department of the body and mind; and at first this may be extremely painful and exceedingly distressing. But suppose you are training the muscles of the body in any particular direction, your muscles become very sore at first, your body will be full of pains; and if you are weak in will and not wisely encouraged to go forward, you may stop right there. But if you will persevere you will soon find that the pain will disappear, and that pleasure and benefit and a more complete use of the body will be the result, and you will say that you never felt better in your life- that you never felt so strong and hearty as now. So when the medium feels a degree of distress and disturbance as the result of his mediumship, it is well to proceed a little further upon the road before you discontinue it. Then after going a little further, and finding no alleviation from distress, but rather an aggravation-finding that the character of the communications is such as rather tends to lead you on a little further and a little further without any appreciable result or satisfaction being obtained- then you will be justified in calling a halt, and demanding of the controlling influences a strict account- make them state definitely what they are going to do. But you should be reasonable in the matter, and not set any limit today that shall harass or hamper them, and allow them plenty of time. When they say they are reasonably sure that such and such things will be accomplished within a certain time, go on and follow the line they have marked out; and if wise and intelligent spirits they will have given such a margin that proof can be given within the stated time that they were accomplishing what they promised. But after the time has elapsed and no progress is made, and no satisfactory reason given on the part of the controls, and the suffering and distress continue, then you would be perfectly justified in saying, 'I have gone so far, I will go no farther; the assurances you have held out to me have not been realized, and I decline to accompany you upon the devious pathway any longer.' You have the right to expect the same honesty and the same straightforwardness and the same intelligent obedience to truth, fact, and law from the inhabitants of the spirit world, that you have from one another living here; spirits have no more right to play the fool with you than you have with one another- and if they come back to you from the spiritual world for the purpose of developing your mediumship, and so undertake a task they are unable to accomplish, the sooner they confess their inability the better. But if in the end success crown their efforts and yours, you will be like the athlete, improved and strengthened in every respect. But at all points and stages of your development, it is your bounden duty to hold the spirits who come to you to a strict accountability for every moment of your time and every ounce of your strength that they occupy or consume.

Q. When spirits enter into a covenant with mortals, will they fulfill their obligations?

A. To the very best of their ability, certainly! But you must bear in mind that spirits are neither infinite nor infallible; they sometimes err through excess of kindness towards you, and at times their desires outrun their discretion. But a spirit that is a thoughtful and intelligent spirit, and who is careful when he makes a promise, like any other rational, sensible being, makes it with the full understanding that he will keep it to the very best of his ability. While such a one cannot guarantee that he absolutely will do so and so, you have a reasonable assurance that it will be accomplished if at all possible. But when a spirit comes to you with a 'Thus saith the Lord,' why then you may congratulate yourself that you have got hold of one of the Wanderers on the Threshold- a person who is probably playing a joke upon you. Place no confidence in such statements. A simple statement with the preface that, using their best endeavors, they hope to be successful in obtaining certain desired results, is worthy of far more attention and trust. It is also well for you to remember that however large the promises of the spirits may be, some duty still remains to you- that you shall help them in the accomplishment of their undertakings.

If you stubbornly resist them and refuse their counsel and their guidance, even to consider it, you can scarcely wonder if, having created the opposition within yourselves, no satisfactory results should follow by and by when the occasion for success arrives.

Q. Speaking of the employments and conditions of spirit life, are those who are mediums here still mediums there, in the sense in which they were mediums here?

A. Not in precisely the same sense, but relatively, yes. There are spheres of spiritual intelligence removed and beyond the first spheres in the spiritual life, even as the first conditions of that life are removed beyond this present one; and the intelligence of the exalted sphere floats down into the life of the sphere beneath it- and this intelligence is expressed through sympathetic and superior minds in the spiritual world, in the same way as intelligence from the spirit-land is imparted to yourselves through the' sympathetic minds that have been attuned, so to speak, or whose natures have been opened to the spiritual world while living here. If mediums in spirit-life desire to take up the labor again and carry forward their duties in that regard, there is ample opportunity for them to do so. But we want you to bear in mind one very important fact here. All the inspired people are not contained within the ranks of Modern Spiritualism; you can find them the world over; among the men of science, in the laboratory of the chemist, in the pulpit; among the authors, the poets, the mechanics, the inventors; among the painters and the dramatists- in the active life of humanity itself. There is inspiration throughout all the domain of human life; and man having a spiritual nature, and that spiritual nature being related to the spiritual world, there is nothing marvelous that the spiritual side of man's nature comes occasionally into harmonious relationship with the realms of spiritual life beyond; while it is perfectly natural that the inspirations from that world should flow down upon man's spirit and be felt and recognized while he lives here. Inspiration is more common and widespread and universal than you suppose; and the inspired speaker of Modern Spiritualism is only the typical illustration of what will be accomplished by man's orderly development in harmony with natural principles, and through the natural operation of the spiritual attributes of man's nature permitting the receiving by him of inspiration from the spiritual world.

Q. Are the spirits pained and grieved by the sufferings and weaknesses of their loved ones on earth?

A. They would scarcely be rational beings if they were not. Death does not destroy their humanity, does not sweep away their sympathy, does not take from them the love they bear to those they have left behind. At first they do not all rise up to that intellectual or spiritual plane that enables them to see beyond the mistakes, and that beyond all these things are smooth waters and fair seas; they see the wrong being done, the error being indulged in, the mistakes that are being continued- and having no wider judgment than the area of the mistake, they suffer sorrow and pain when those they love do wrong and suffer from their weaknesses. But when they unfold to see beyond the present evil, and see the results of law and principles of operation, they learn that they are in some way benefits- that the soul must pass through them to attain to higher and better things- and accept it as a part and parcel of the purposes of the Eternal in relation to the progress of humanity. But they feel if these things can be avoided, if man can be taught to travel an easier road- the road to happiness through righteousness rather than through wrongfulness, through right and justice rather than shame and suffering and misdoing- they desire to do all in their power to accomplish this result. But they know that no matter how deep are the wrongs that now pertain to their loved ones, and that though they will have to be atoned for in the future, they' are but temporary, and will surely yet give place to the law of eternal right and justice. They learn that in the end eternity is long enough for every tangled web of evil and wrong-doing to be straightened out, and for all of these dark places to be made plain.

Q. I have a letter from an old Spiritualist, and would like to have the Control answer the objections contained in one paragraph which I will read: "Spiritualism is a truth, but its phenomena utterly fail to make its believers better, truer, and purer men and women; on the contrary, the tendency is in the other direction. I speak prom an experience 35 years in it. Not that Spiritualists are worse than others, but the system and practice of mediumship, the necessary surrender of one's individuality to others, 'the Lord knows who,' is of itself degrading, belittling, and demoralizing." What can you say to that?

A. We have but very little to say, though we could say very much. A belief in the phenomena of Spiritualism will never do any one any real moral or spiritual good; but belief in the phenomena of Spiritualism, as the result of intelligent and morally-responsible agents, may do a great deal of good to the individual, as a means of determining the character of the life beyond; and it will, in time, become the potent element of a great moral revolution which will induce a spiritual upheaval of human nature that shall ultimately place mankind upon the highest plane of individual and personal righteousness. But we have not reached the spiritual development of this exalted position; therefore a consideration now must be had as to another point raised by the good friend. The effect of the surrender of the individual will to the judgment of any spirit, 'the Lord knows who,' is in itself degrading and repulsive.

We perfectly agree with our friend, and entirely endorse the statement, and say that here is one of the barriers of personal progress in Spiritualism among mediums and Spiritualists. Whenever you surrender your judgment and your will to any one, 'the Lord knows who,' that comes from the spiritual world, you are doing precisely the thing you would not do to any human being that you happened to encounter in this world; and if any 'the Lord knows who' were to happen to meet you on the street, and say 'come with me and take a ride across the Bay, or take a ride on this car,' you would at once want to know who he was, and what he wanted you to do this for; and until he had satisfied you as to who he was and what his intentions were, you would be very likely to decline to join him. When there comes to you 'the Lord knows who,' and he says, 'I am a spirit; you must go to this town and preach, you must work here, you must go to that house and say that they must accept the angelic messenger,' and you straightway go and do as you are bid, you will realize the painful experience that a surrender of the judgment and will to 'the Lord knows who' is very degrading and belittling. But suppose the spirit to be a person in whom you used to have implicit confidence while living here, suppose that person so clearly demonstrated the continuity of his own life that you have no doubt that it is the same individual, and that person says to you that he wants to advise you, counsel with you, and suggests that you do this or the other thing- you, knowing his advice and counsel were good while he lived in this world, will be prepared and willing to give heed to him. But, as here in this world, you will not entirely surrender your reason and judgment to him; and if he is an honest ghost, he will ask you to weigh his counsel by your own reason and observation. This is very different from an entire surrender of your reason and your judgment to somebody, 'the Lord knows who.' The surrender of the judgment and reason and personal will has been the fruitful cause of three-fourths of the misery that has been associated with the development of mediumship; it is a doctrine that can never result satisfactorily in the great majority of cases; here and there exceptional and peculiar circumstances may temporarily warrant it; but, plainly and emphatically, let us put it that when mediumship demands the surrender of reason and intelligence, and makes a man or woman less a man or woman for being a medium than they would have been without being a medium, then surrender the mediumship, assert your manhood and womanhood; for an honest man and an honest woman are a great deal more useful to this world than the most brilliant mediumship that sacrifices every element of moral and personal character in its development and operation.

Q. Is there any rule for the development of clairvoyance?

A. A dozen different rules may be stated, and each one may utterly fail, while the thirteenth may accomplish all that is desired. The simplest rule we can give you is this: for one hour a day seclude yourself from all your fellows, and first try closing the eyes and meditating internally, thus shutting out all external thoughts as far as possible; and by and by, with a little practice, you will be able to dismiss them from you altogether. Then, when you have succeeded in establishing that condition of internal communion and meditation with yourself, definitely direct your mind to some especial thing. To do this easily it is better to place a bandage across the eyes- a soft, silken bandage will assist you quite as well, especially if it be black; place it directly over the eyes, and fasten it at the base of the brain, and direct the mind to a clock or picture that may hang in the room. At first you may find it difficult indeed, and you may perceive no indication of development; but after a few trials, probably five or six, the eyes may begin to recognize streaks of light shooting across the sight, and there may be pains affecting the brow and perhaps the eye itself, and the mind will seem to be centered in the eye for the purpose of seeing. Persevere- keep the mind continually fixed upon what you want accomplished. Do not make the thought too intense, but make it persistent; and in a few weeks' time you will be able to perceive, dimly at first, in miniature, the clock or article you are trying to see, and you will presently be able to state the time it indicates. When you are able to perceive the clock and first catch a glimpse of it, and are perfectly sure of the fact, then remove the bandage, and see if what you supposed to be the time is correct. You will then be able to verify the experiment itself. It may happen that you have seen the watch inverted, and the very opposite of the time you state will be presented. Remember that little point. But not alone quietude of mind and internal meditation are necessary; there are other things required as well. The first is perfect cleanliness of the body; the second is the most perfect cleanliness of mind; and the third, and most important of all, the most perfect cleanliness in diet. All these are necessary to successfully unfold the latent clairvoyance.

You must refuse all stimulants and narcotics and all flesh diet, living upon plain and simple foods, giving strict attention to bodily and mental conditions. It may be necessary for you to be magnetized, and some genial friend or acquaintance in whom you have confidence may be able to materially assist you. After you have discovered that you can develop these latent spiritual powers, then you have to determine in what way or direction the future development shall be exercised; this is an important point that you need to consider carefully, and you should pursue that course in which the development seems to be the strongest and most natural.

Q. Should children sit for development?

A. As a general thing we discountenance the development of children as mediums. Our observation is, that mediumship should never be developed until the physical system has nearly attained its growth. You can then draw upon the vitality of the system without much danger to the health of body or mind of the individual. Certainly we should say, not before seventeen or eighteen years of age; and if the attempt at development is put off even two years longer, the individual would certainly profit greatly by it, and lose nothing. It is most pernicious physiologically and spiritually to try to hasten the development in any case in growing children; they will become bodily and mentally demoralized, to use a common expression; and we warn you in no case to undertake to develop your children in such a manner until they have reached the period referred to, when they will have a supply of reserve force, so to speak, to fall back upon. From eighteen to forty years, in the meridian of life, is the best period for the development of mediumship; and the best period of all, in the majority of cases, is from twenty-five to thirty-five years of age.

Q. What is the indication where a person sees, after closing the eyes, what they have been observing before the eyes were closed?

A. It is the perfect impression of the object upon the retina, just the last impression, and is reproduced as a sort of subjective panorama, a sort of camera obscura; by the closing of the eye, a photographic image is recorded on the optic nerve.

Q. Sometimes we say this person has a gift for this or that; is it a gift from the spiritual sources, or is it in the nature of the individual?

A. It is in their own nature, in every case. The spiritual world can give you nothing. God has endowed you all with the same latent abilities, and the circumstances of life determine the quality and development in every case. The spiritual world may assist you in bringing out that which is contained in yourselves.

Q. Spirits that have never had earthly experience of any length of time, when they come back to identify themselves to their relatives or friends, what is the effect upon that spirit in spirit life? Is it beneficial or otherwise, and is it requisite that that spirit should have some experience through a sensitive on the earth plane?

A. There are two very important questions involved in this most exceedingly interesting subject. For instance, the spirits who enter into the spiritual world prematurely, to use the language of earth, enter in from one of three causes: either as a consequence of the willful operation of the mother, through foeticide, through some malpractice or injury of the human system, or through certain laws having terminated the possibility of their physical existence in this world. In the first case it is scarcely reasonable to suppose that the individual spirit is likely to derive large personal benefit from contact with its mother; but here another interesting point is involved which will have to be considered. Many a woman who has taken this unwise course feels, when this has been accomplished, waves of sorrow and regret sweep over her, and she would give all the years of her life if this thing could not have been. Now suppose a little spirit growing and developing comes back again into the mortal sphere, and the mother is made aware of that fact, why the floodgates of her soul would be opened, and such a psychological disturbance would come forth as would do that child an infinite amount of harm and mischief for the time being.

Therefore it is that wise guardians in spirit life take charge of such waifs,, and keep them in their surroundings and develop them spiritually, and build them up in a manner that avoids the necessity of their being brought again in contact with the material sphere they originally sprang from. Such are sometimes brought into the sphere of human activity, brought to observe the condition of material life through the influence and experience of others, and they gain a practical knowledge of the world they have been so unceremoniously ejected from. But it is not absolutely necessary that they should be brought back into this world, because the grand army of humanity passes from it and carries a sufficiency of experience forward with them into the spiritual world to be an abundant means of instruction; and these who carry with them much of the earth conditions are selected by wise teachers to take these waifs in charge. When a physiological law has been violated, as in premature birth and consequent death, then, of necessity, the moral and spiritual conditions are very different to the first case. In this instance, welling up with its love, the mother sphere unfolding in the spiritual nature, there is a point of contact with the spiritual thought that is in the spiritual world; and the two blending in harmony and unity, the mother love flows out with sweet affection to the babe and thrills its inmost soul to the center, and it is drawn to the mother by it. Thus there are many interesting problems involved in this question, as well as many suggestions. One conclusion we will draw from it: there is one crime against yourself that will stand out before you in the spiritual world as a dreadful guilt, and that crime is the premature ejection into spiritual existence of that which should be the pride and glory of your manhood and womanhood.

Q. At what stage of the growth and development of the child, prior to its birth in this world, is it immortal?

A. The immortality of the child is coincident with conception itself; therefore, at any stage of the subsequent development, if it is interfered with, there is the fact of the attempted demolition of a human life. But the essential element of it, nevertheless, still continues, will still be manifest, and grow and unfold.

CLOSING REMARKS BY THE CONTROL

We have to thank you most heartily, friends, for the spiritual and fraternal sympathy and support you have accorded us from night to night, during this course of Advanced Class-meetings; and in leaving you now with our present duties concluded, with great and joyous feelings in our hearts that we have met Upon the common plane of mutual desire to gain knowledge, we invoke the blessing of the highest and best upon each and everyone of you, and trust that the light that has been gleaming in your souls may become a strong and growing flame of divine radiance in the future. May your days be full of usefulness and beauty, and when the time comes for you to march forward to that greater and better realm beyond, may you be filled with the sublime and peaceful consciousness that you have endeavored to do your best at all times; and then it shall truly be said of you, even as you will permit us in all humbleness to say of ourselves, 'We have done our best, the wisest can do no more, nor should the poorest do less.' May the truth and justice of eternal righteousness and knowledge be with you and keep you henceforth and forevermore.

THE END

Made in the USA
Lexington, KY
26 February 2019